Nataliya Zabolotna

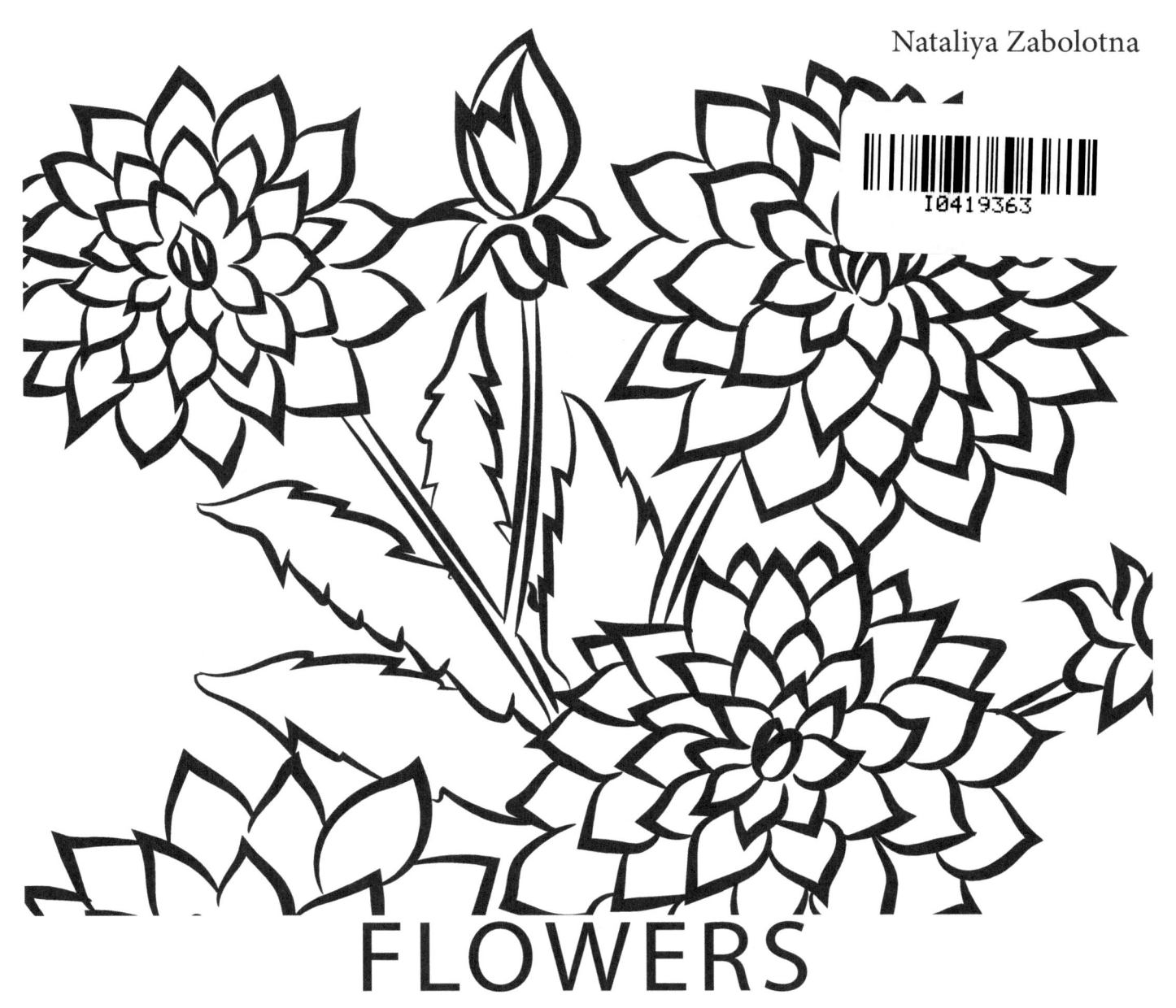

FLOWERS

COLORING BOOK

BEAUTIFUL PICTURES

FOR ADULTS

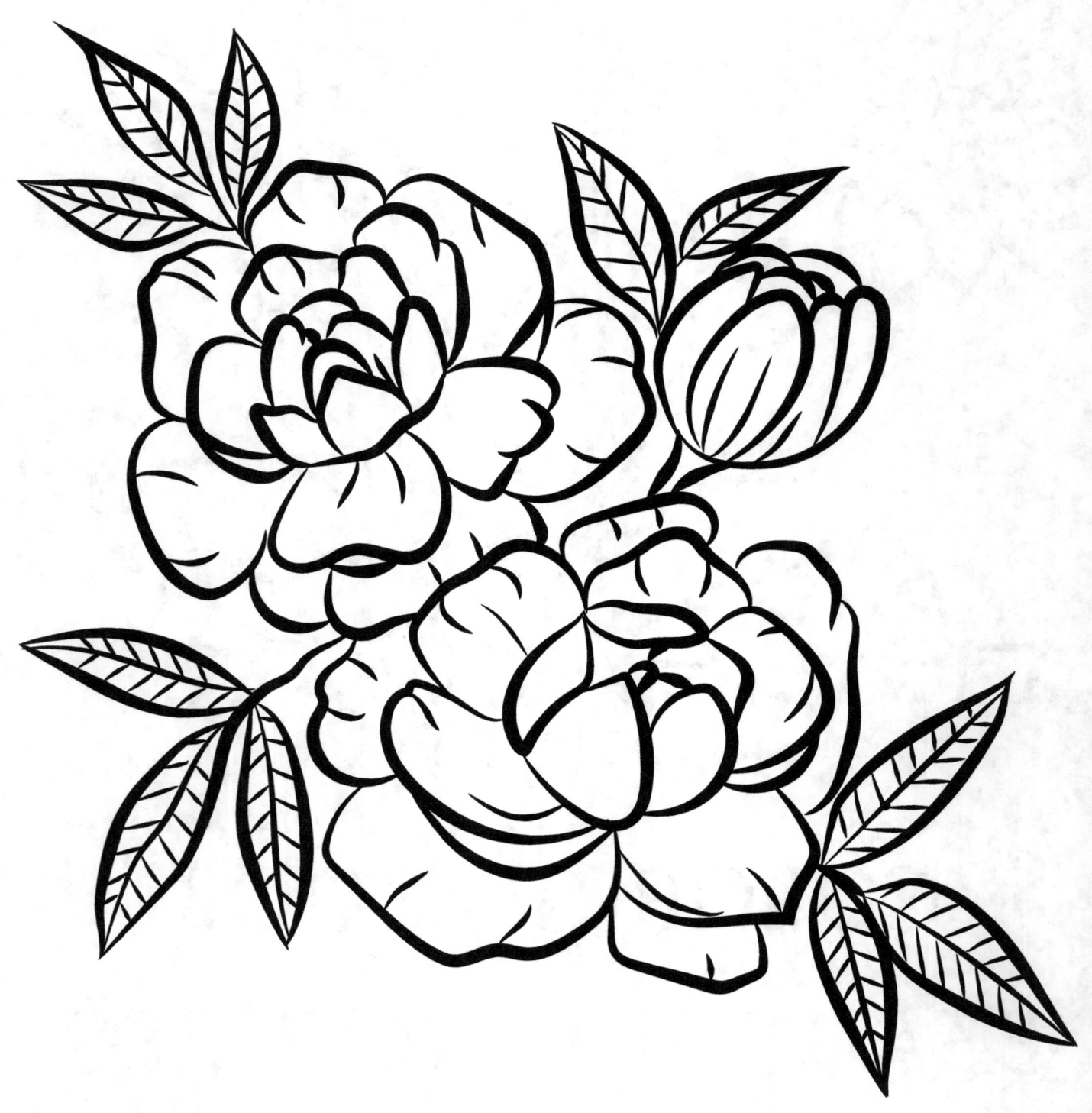

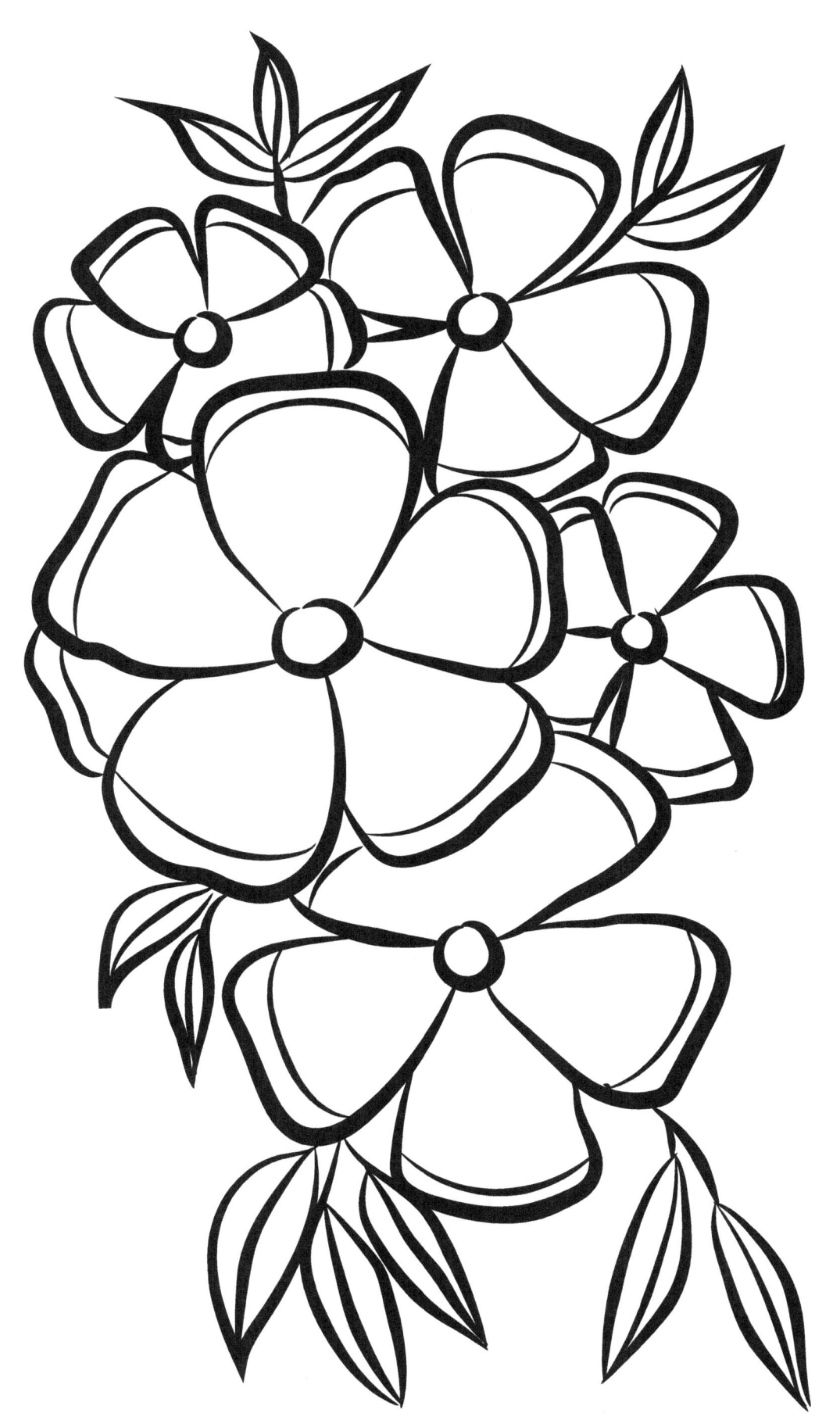

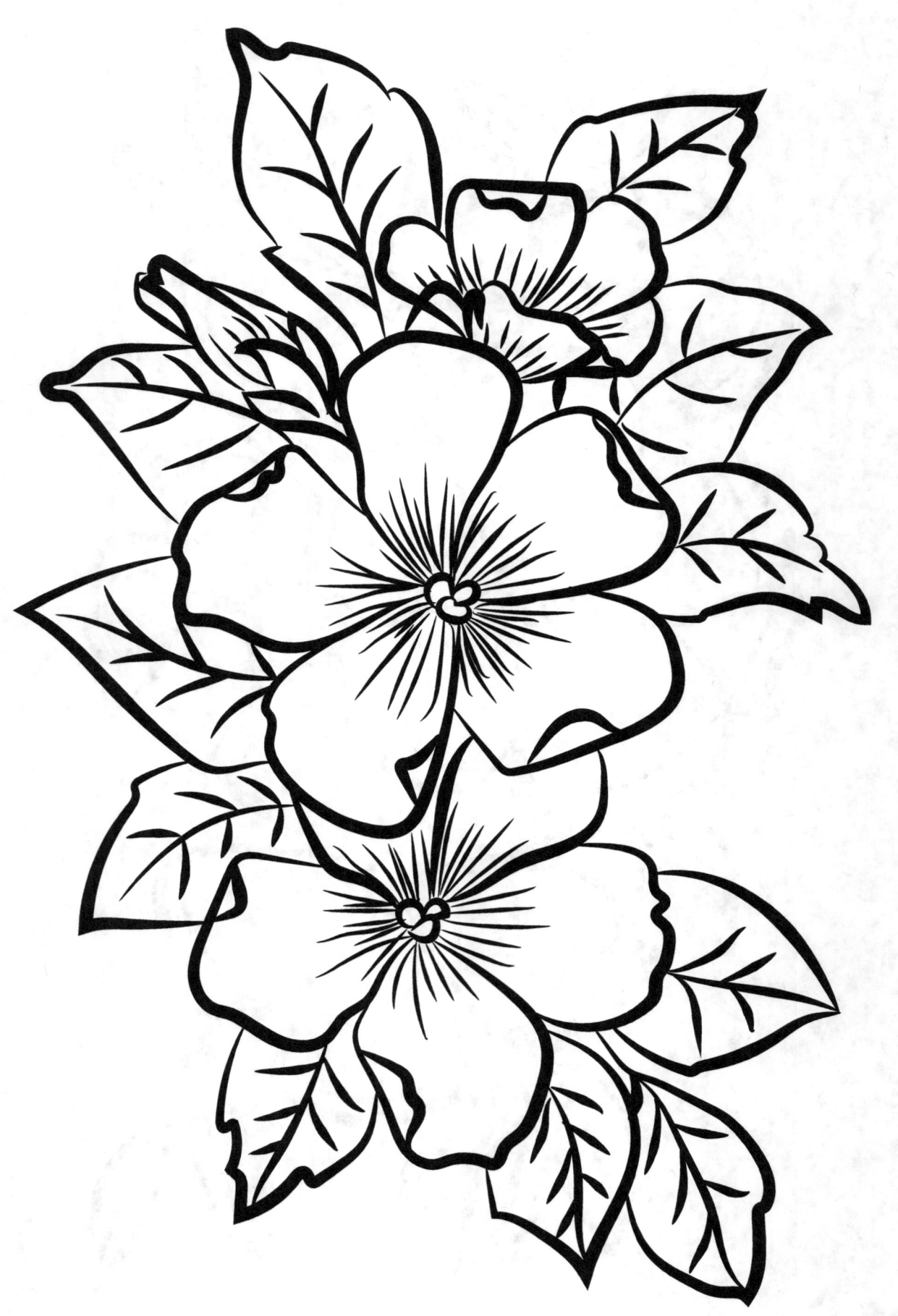

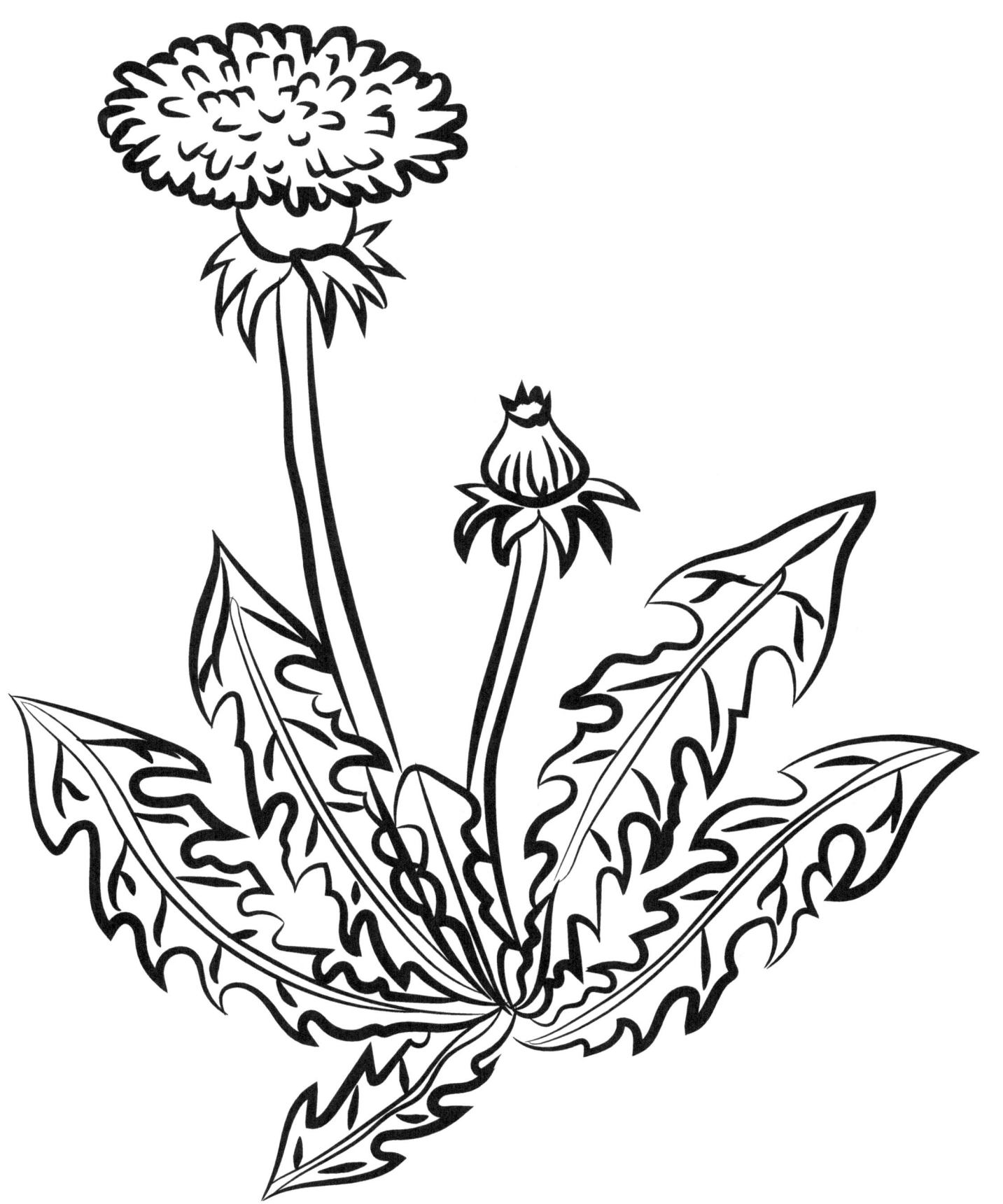

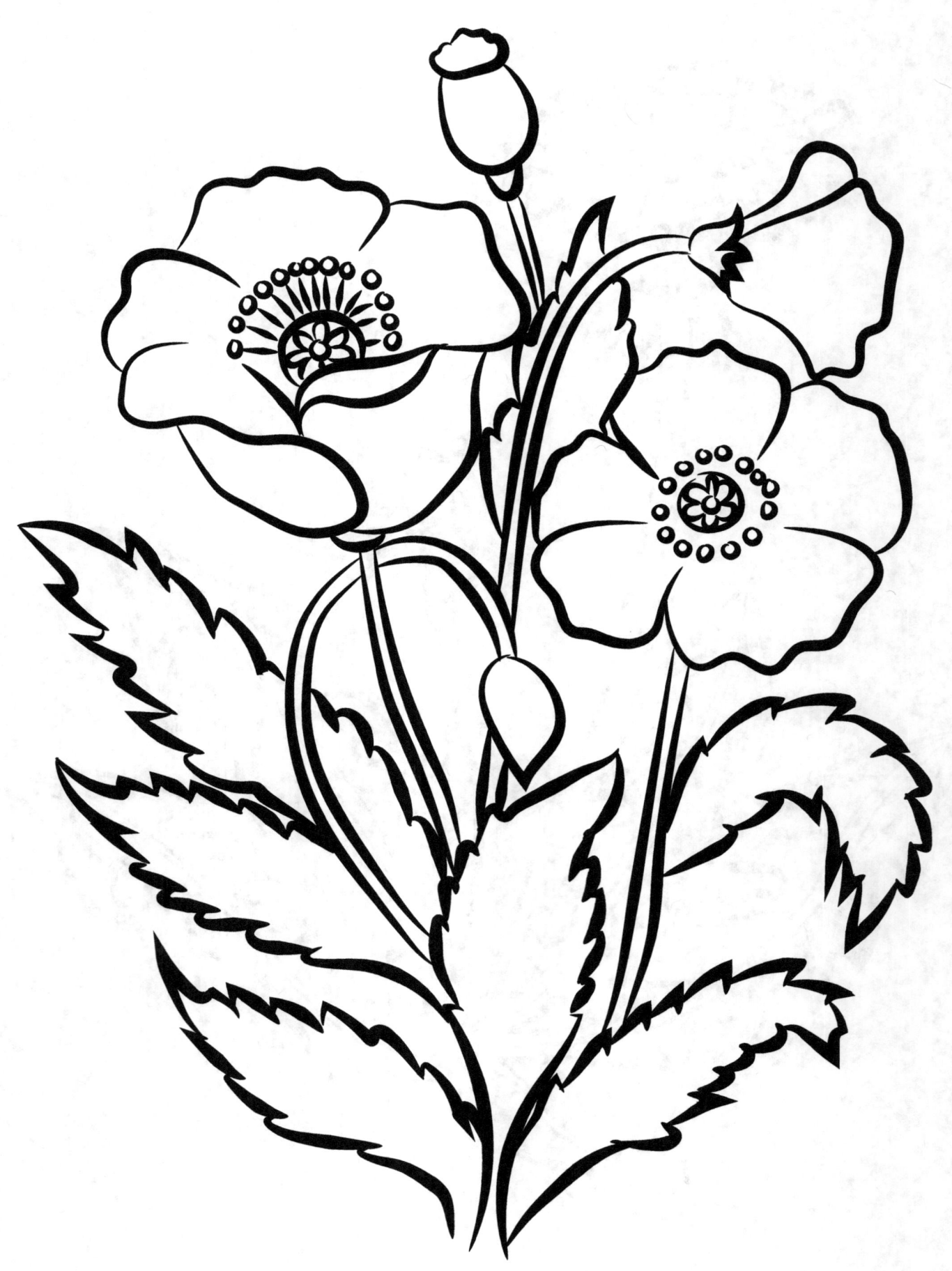

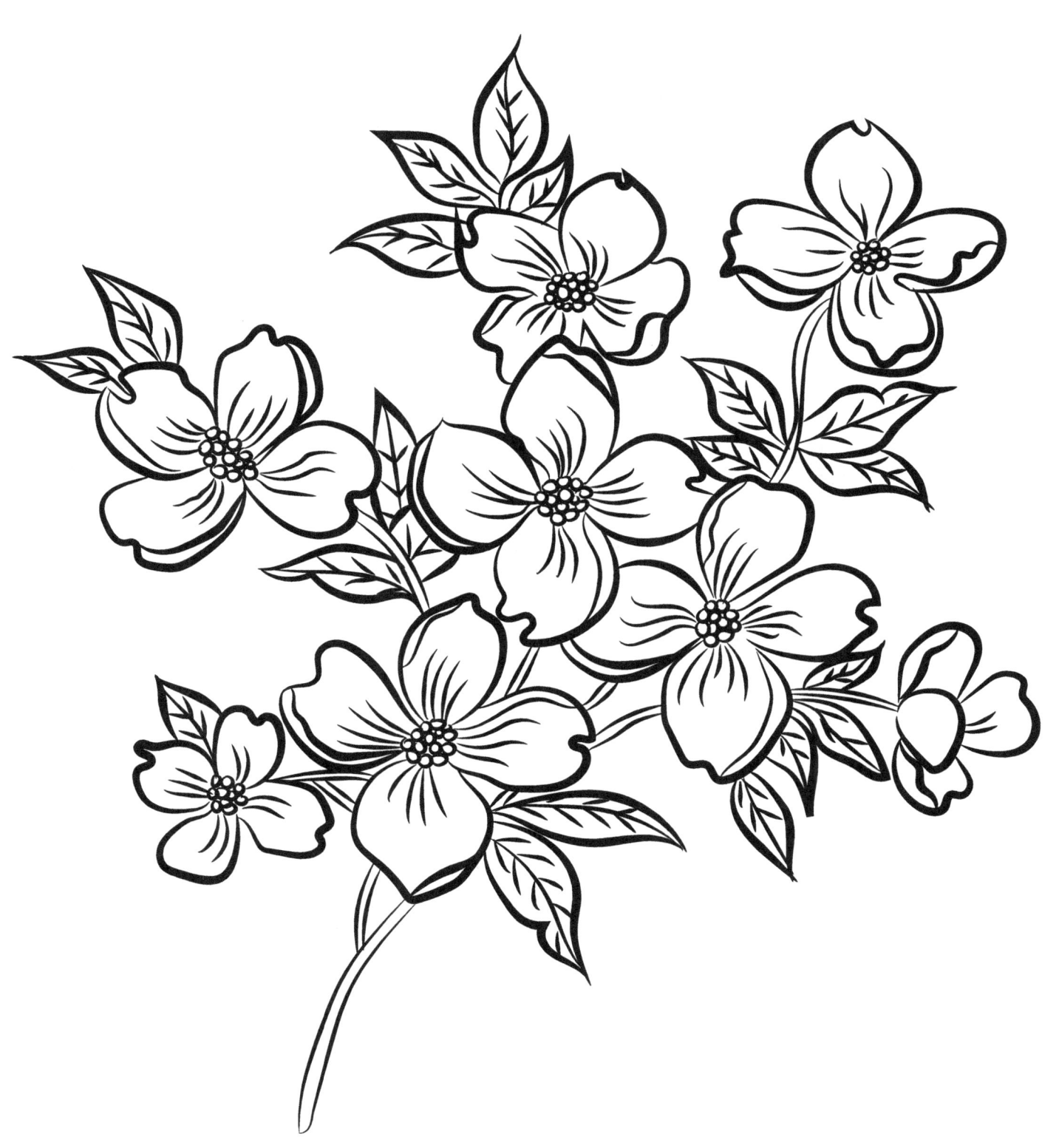

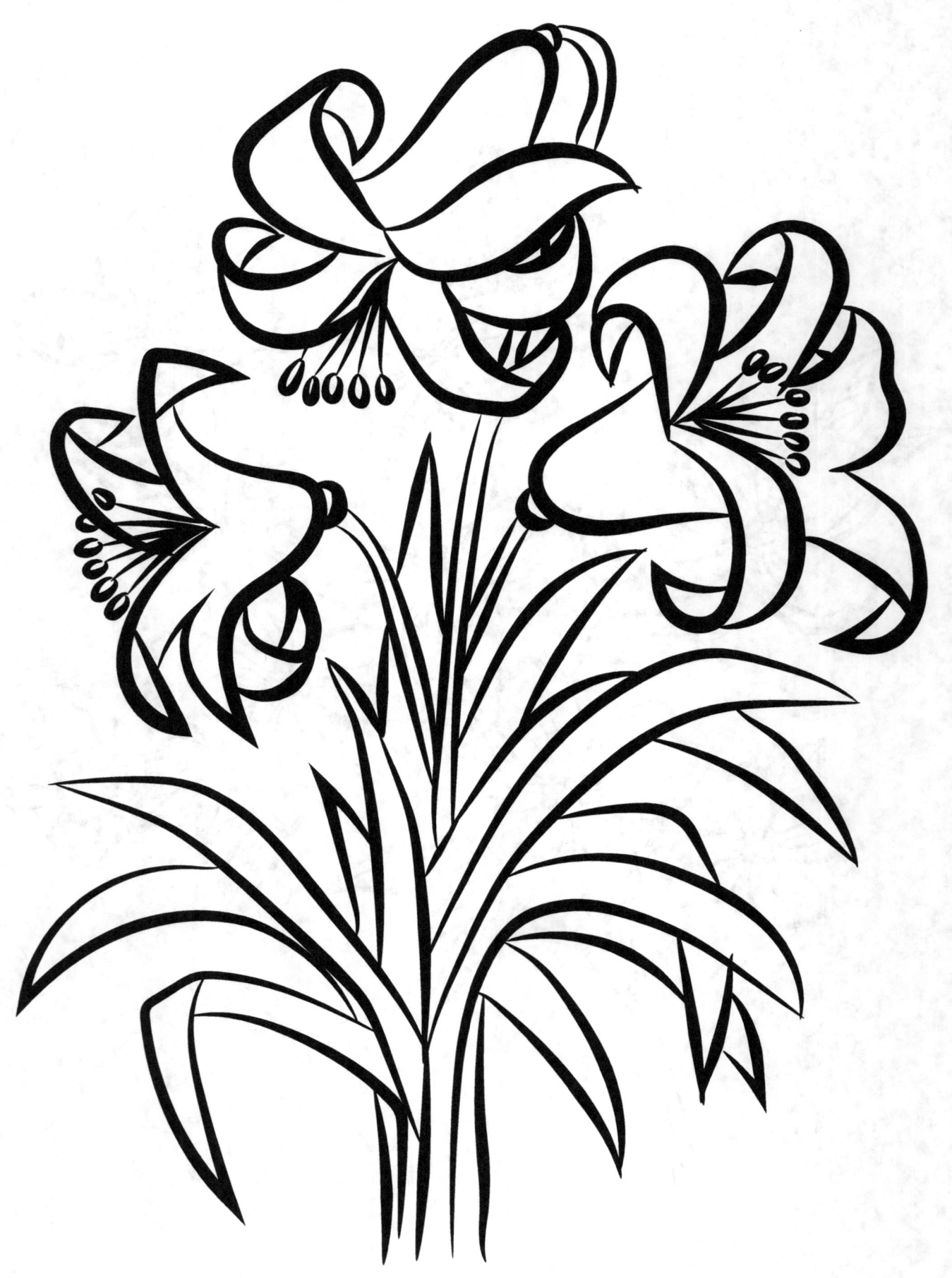

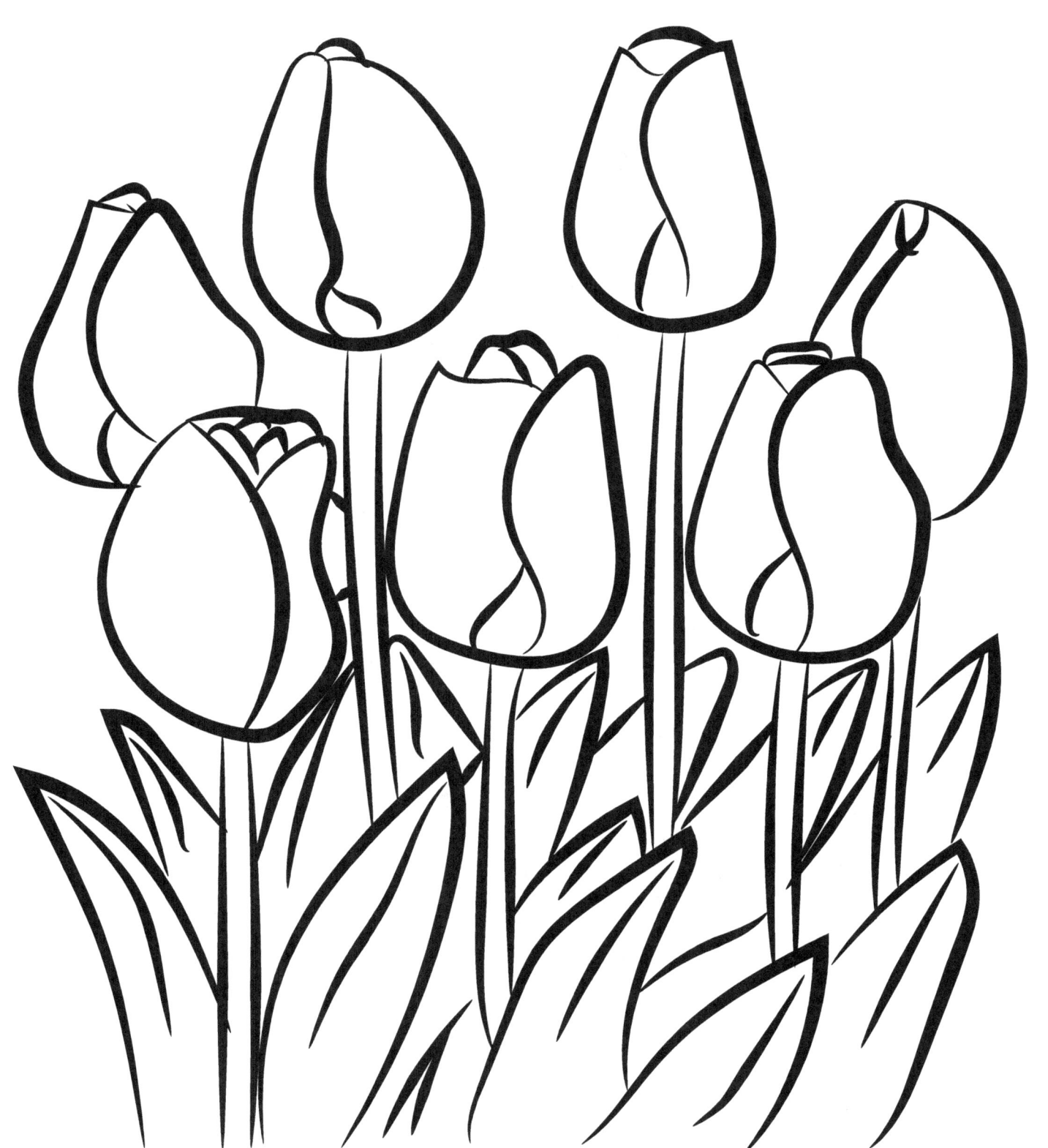

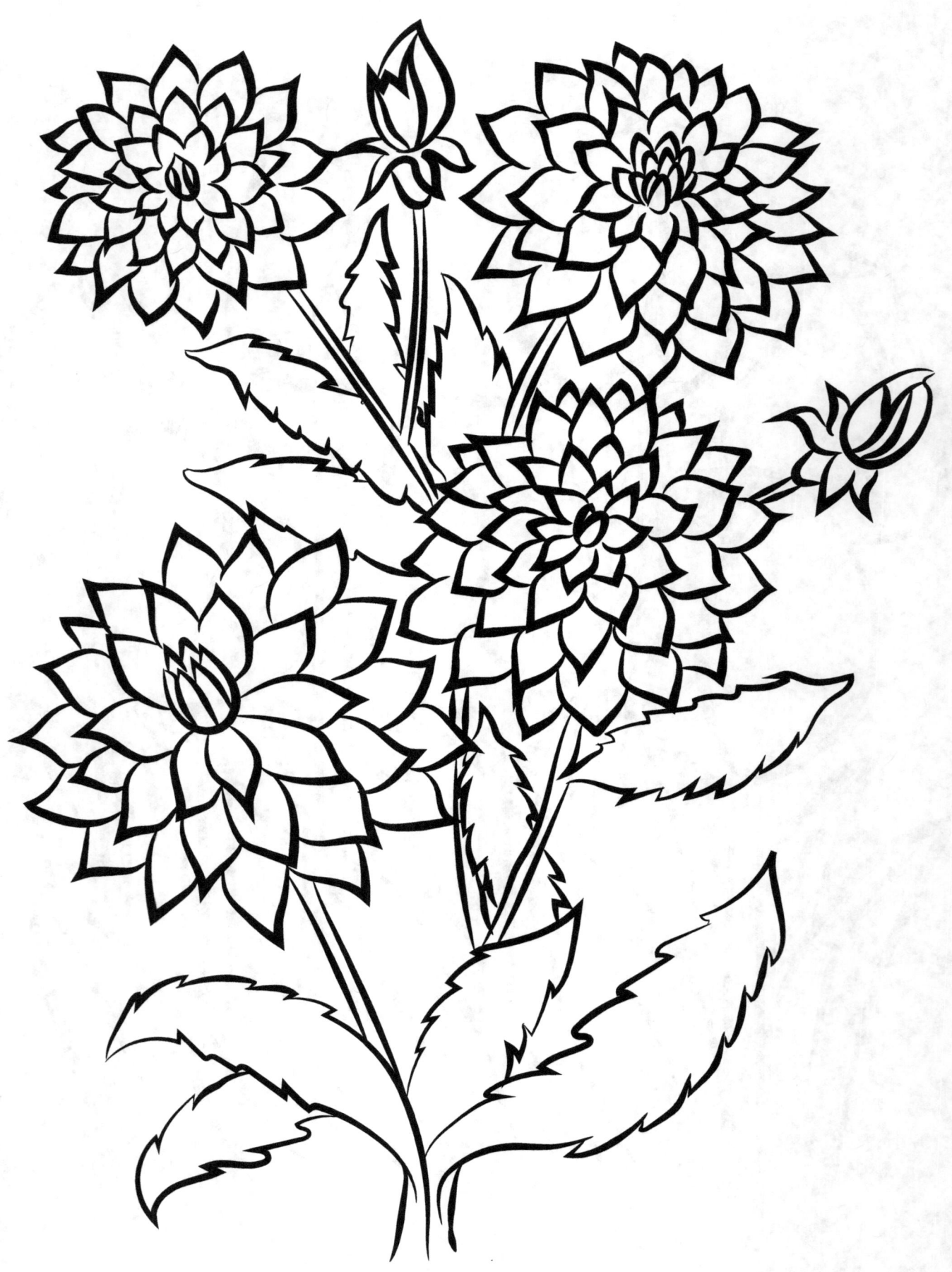

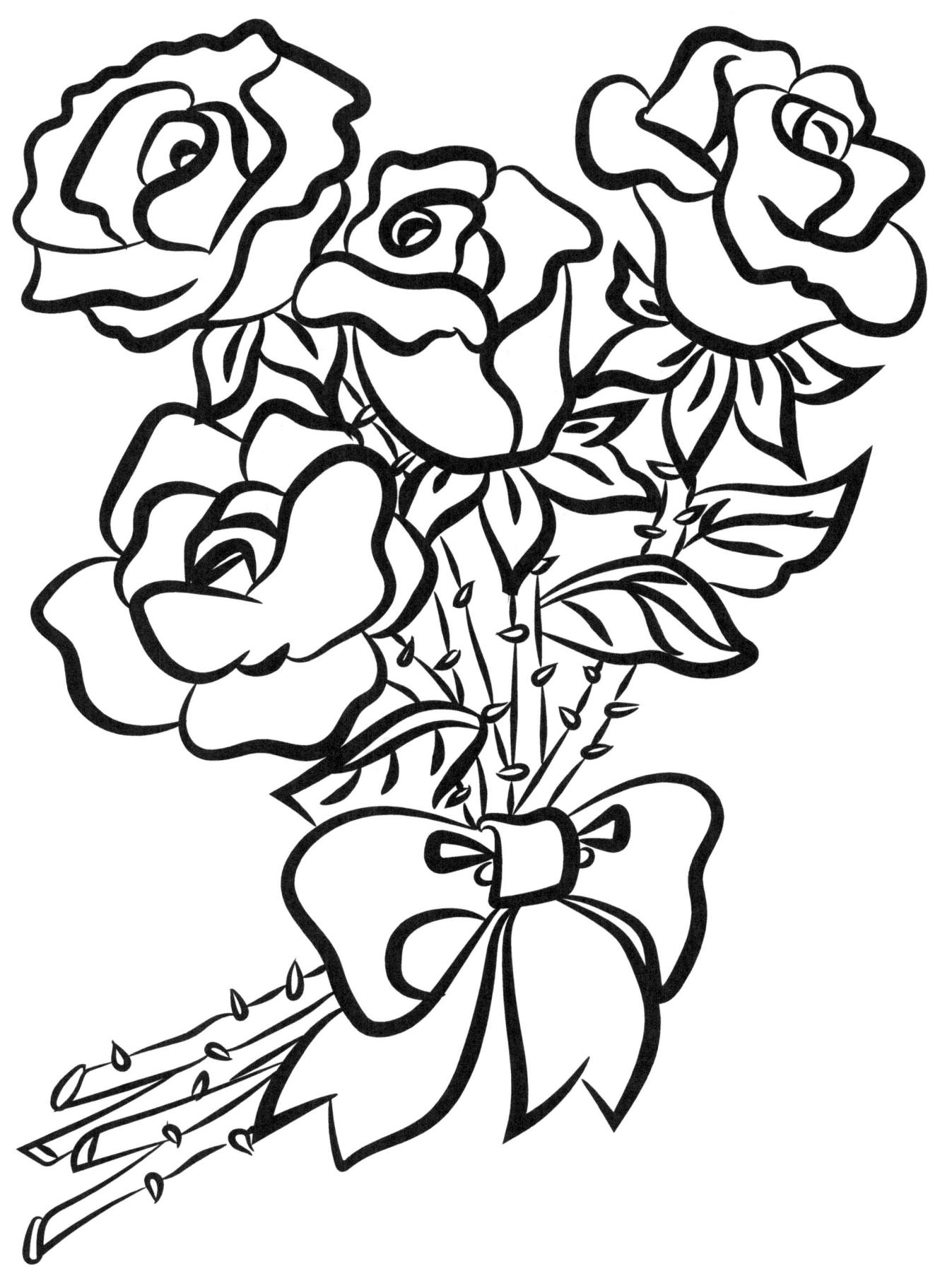

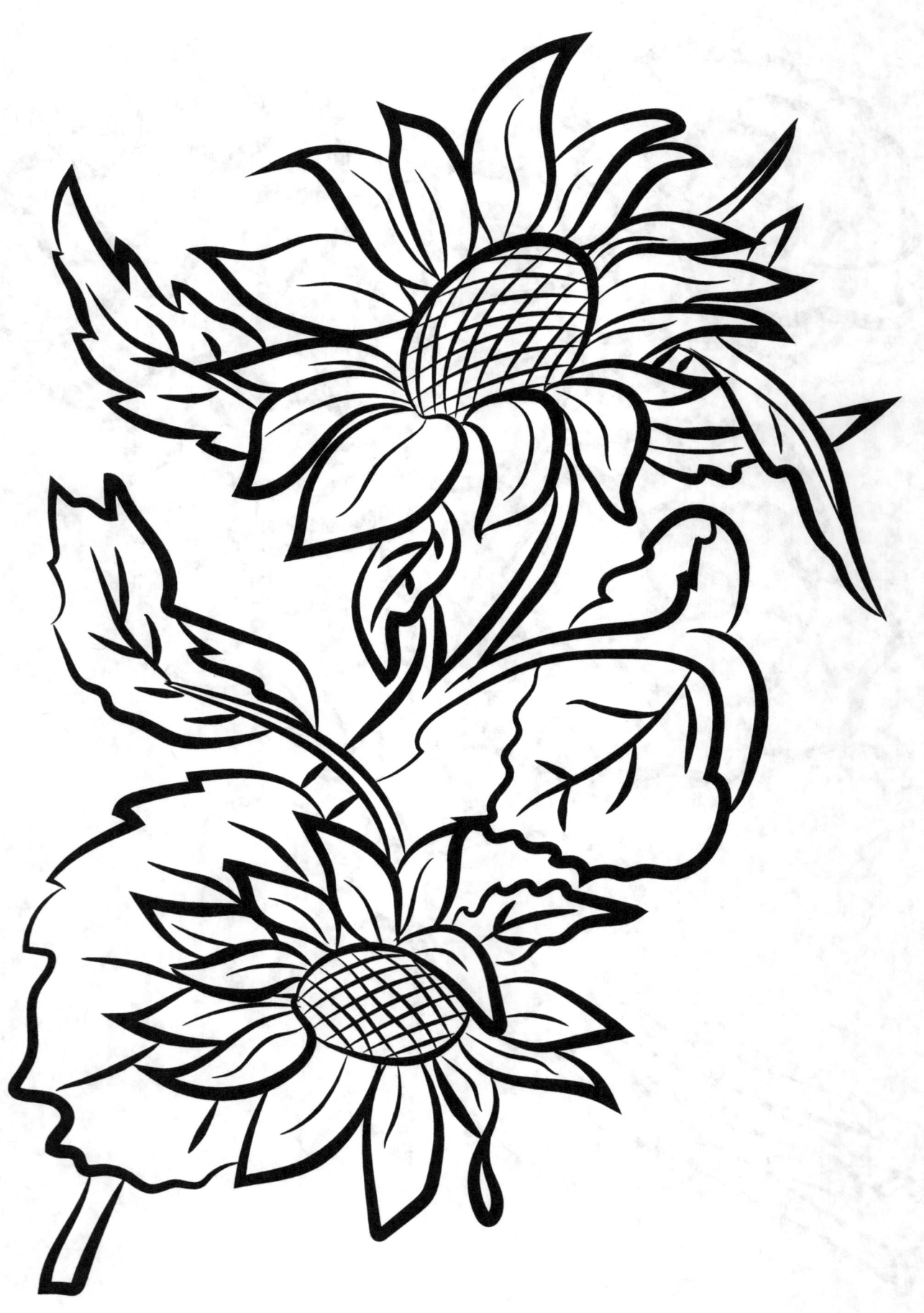

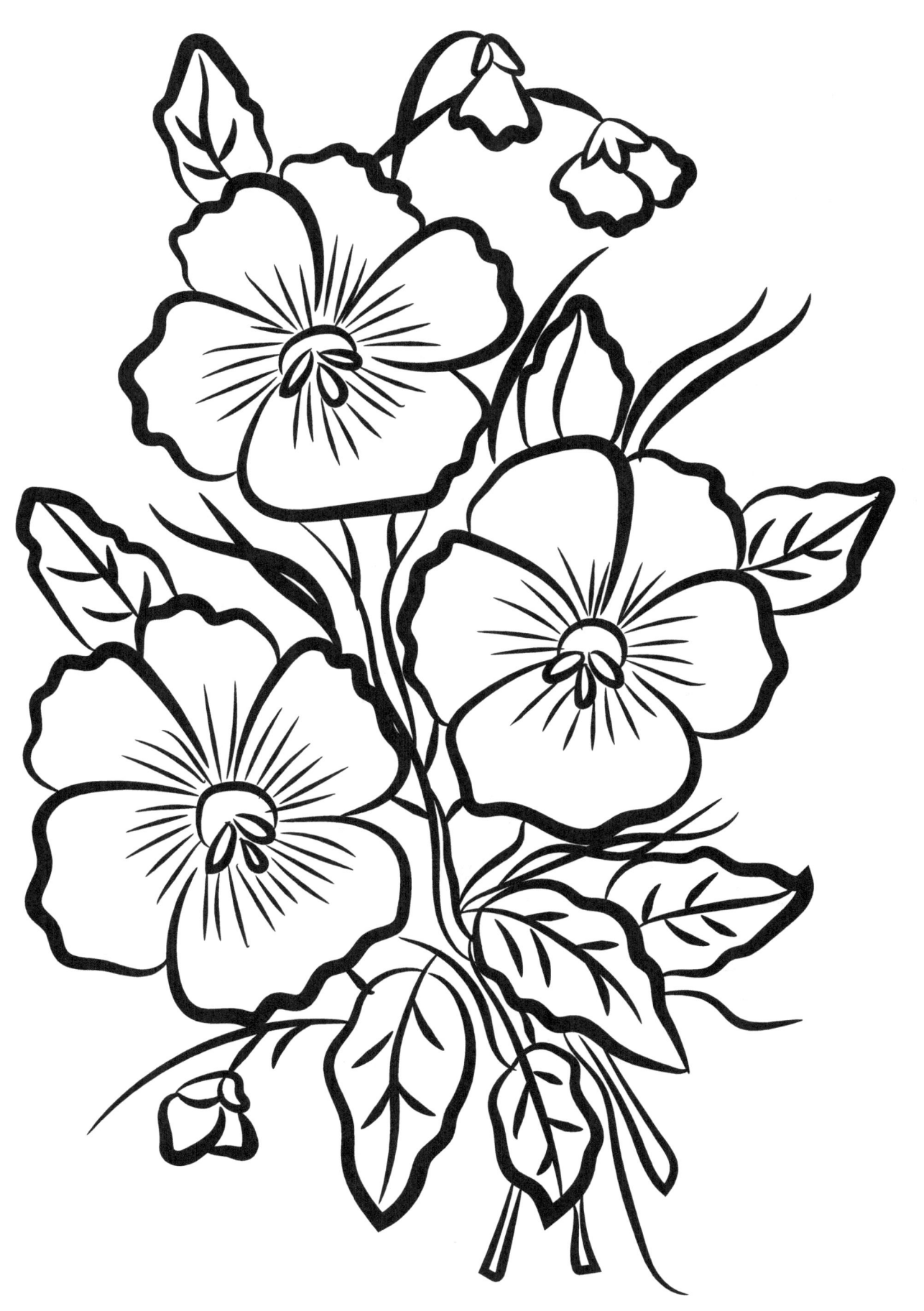

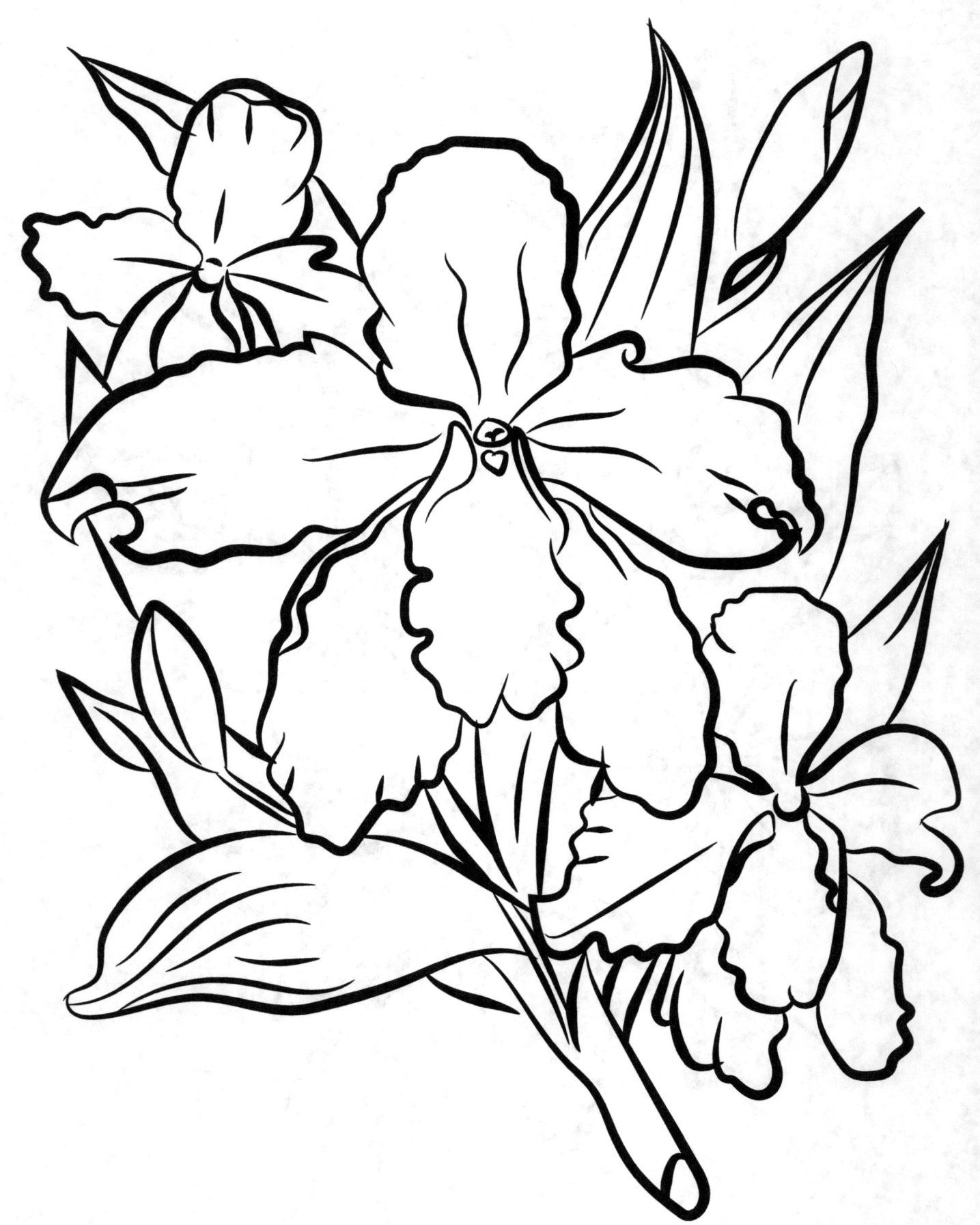

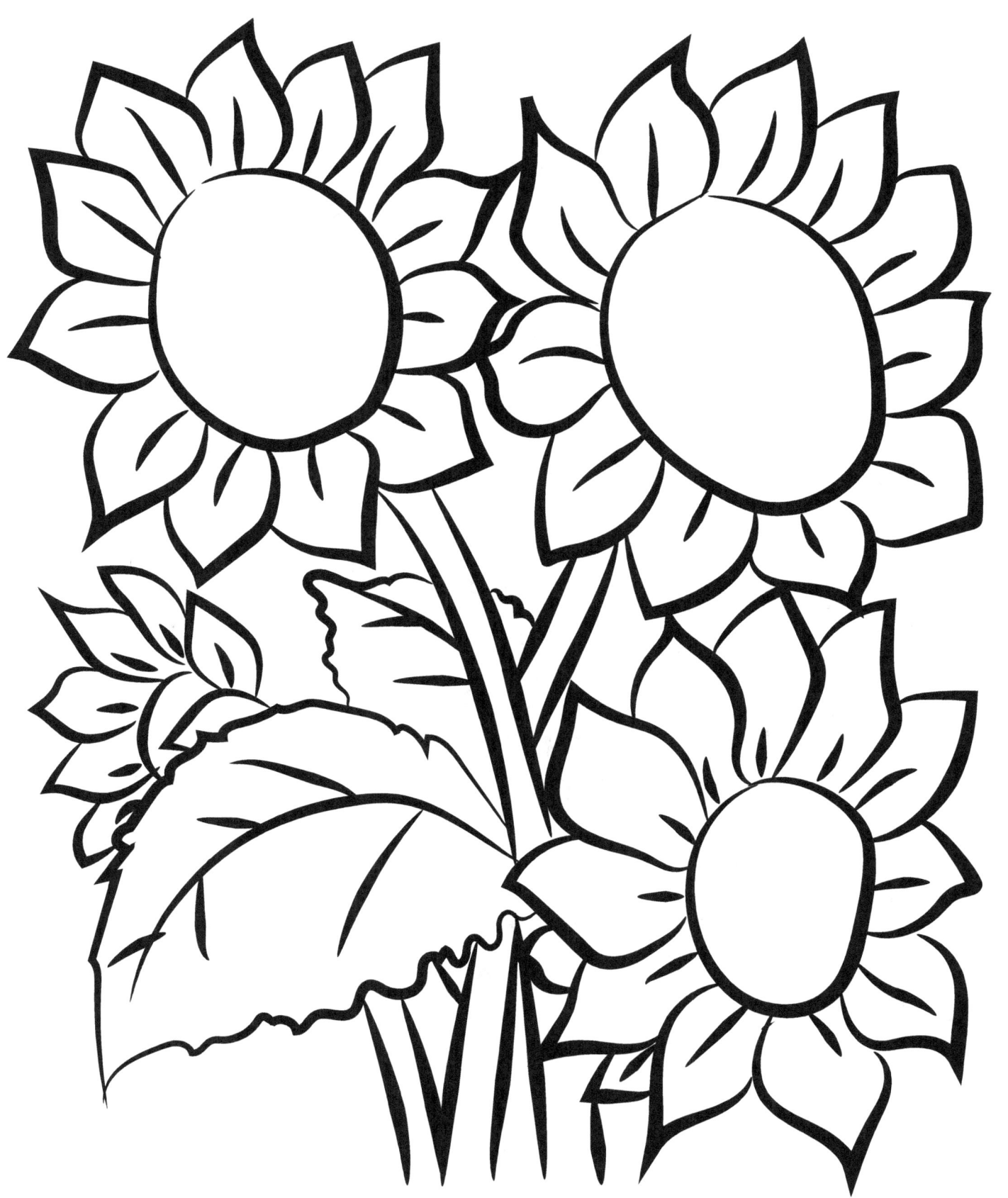

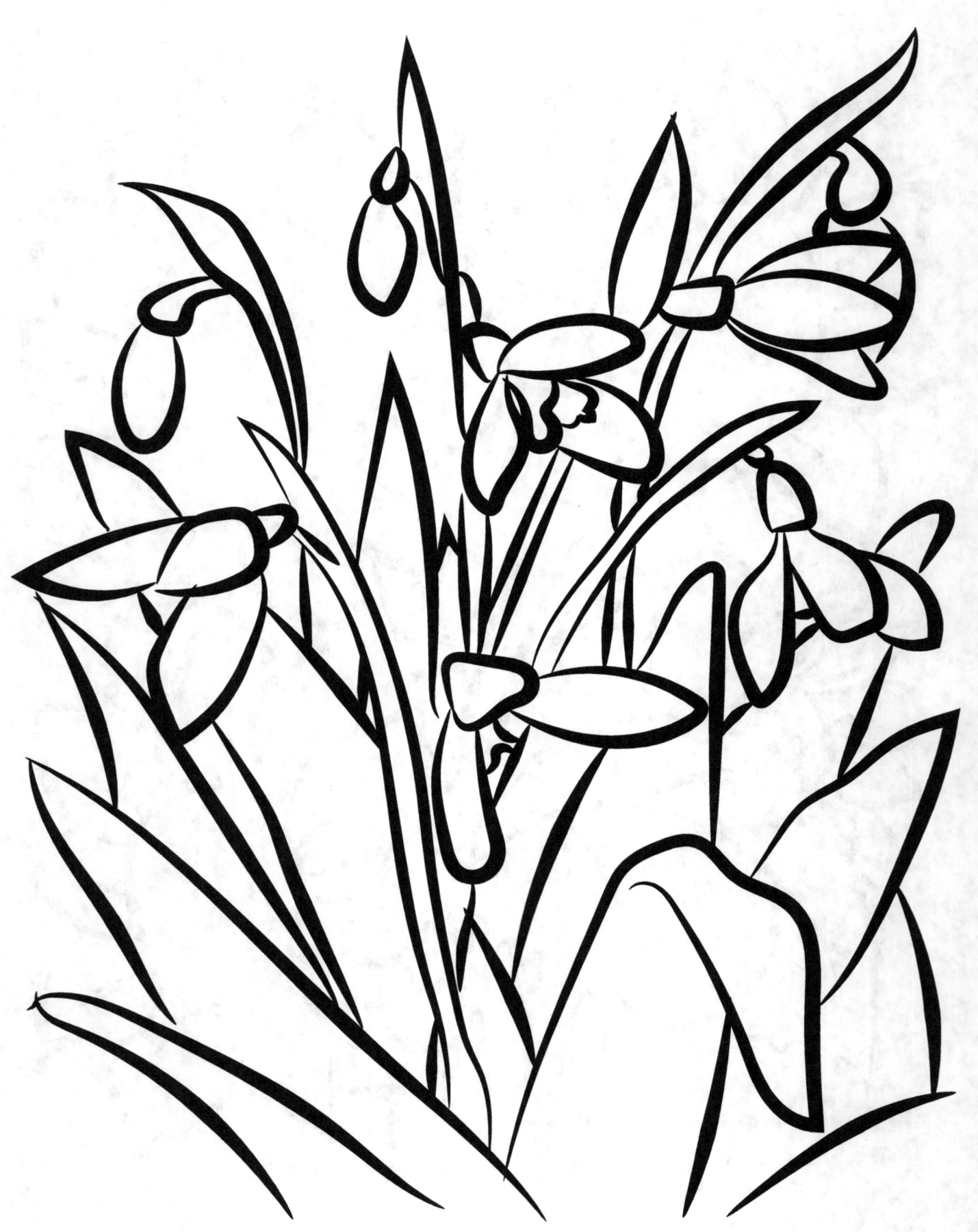

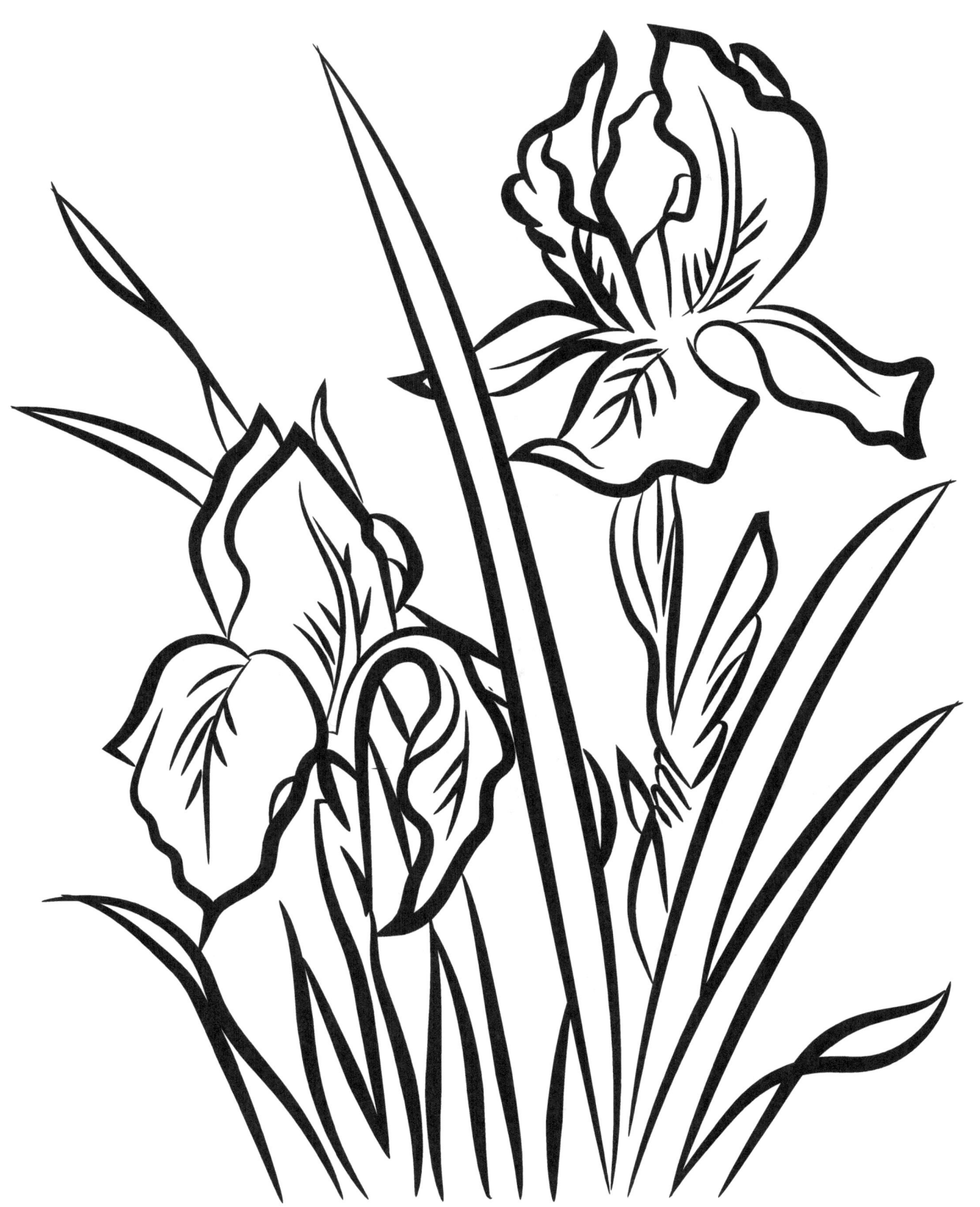

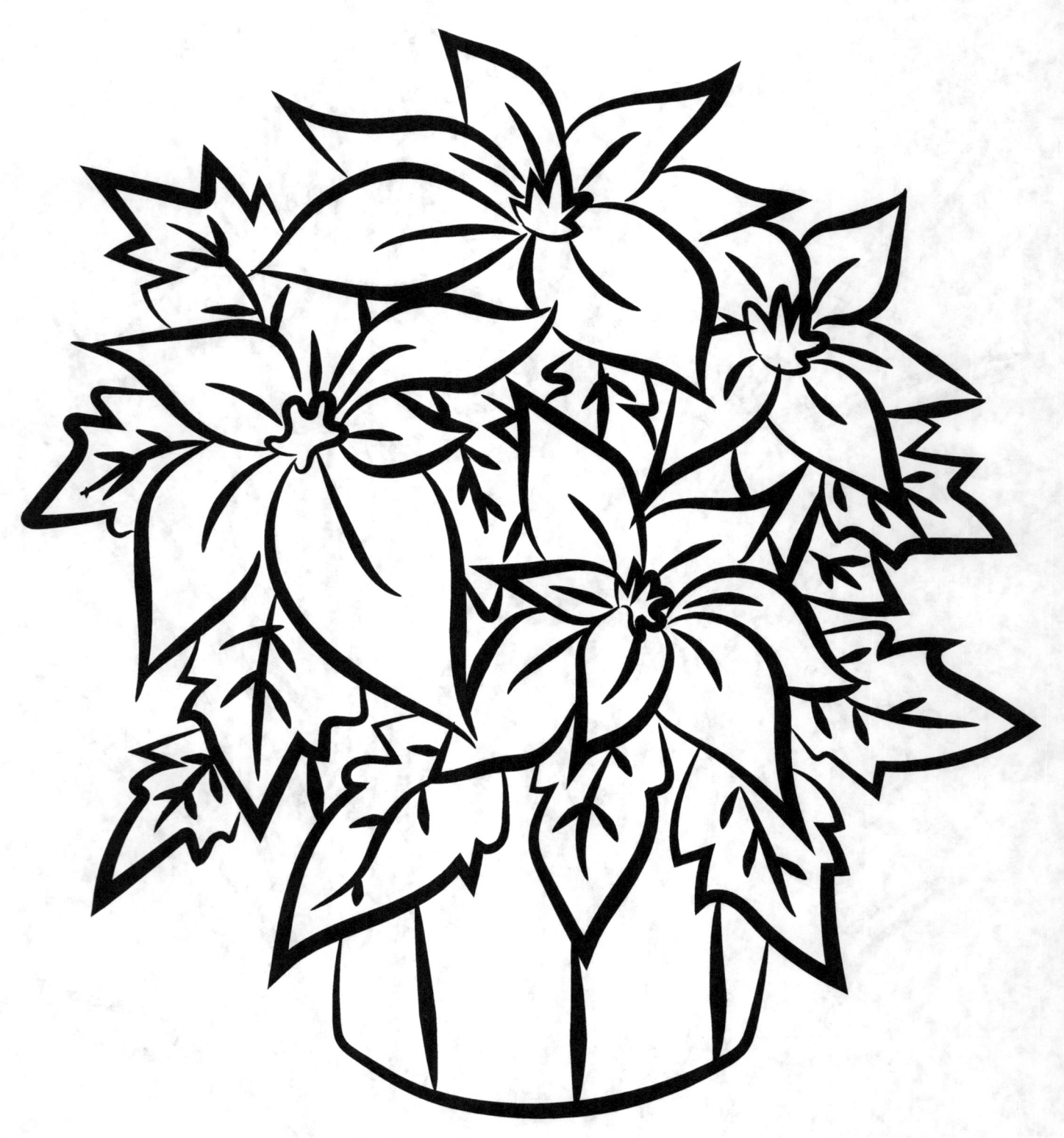

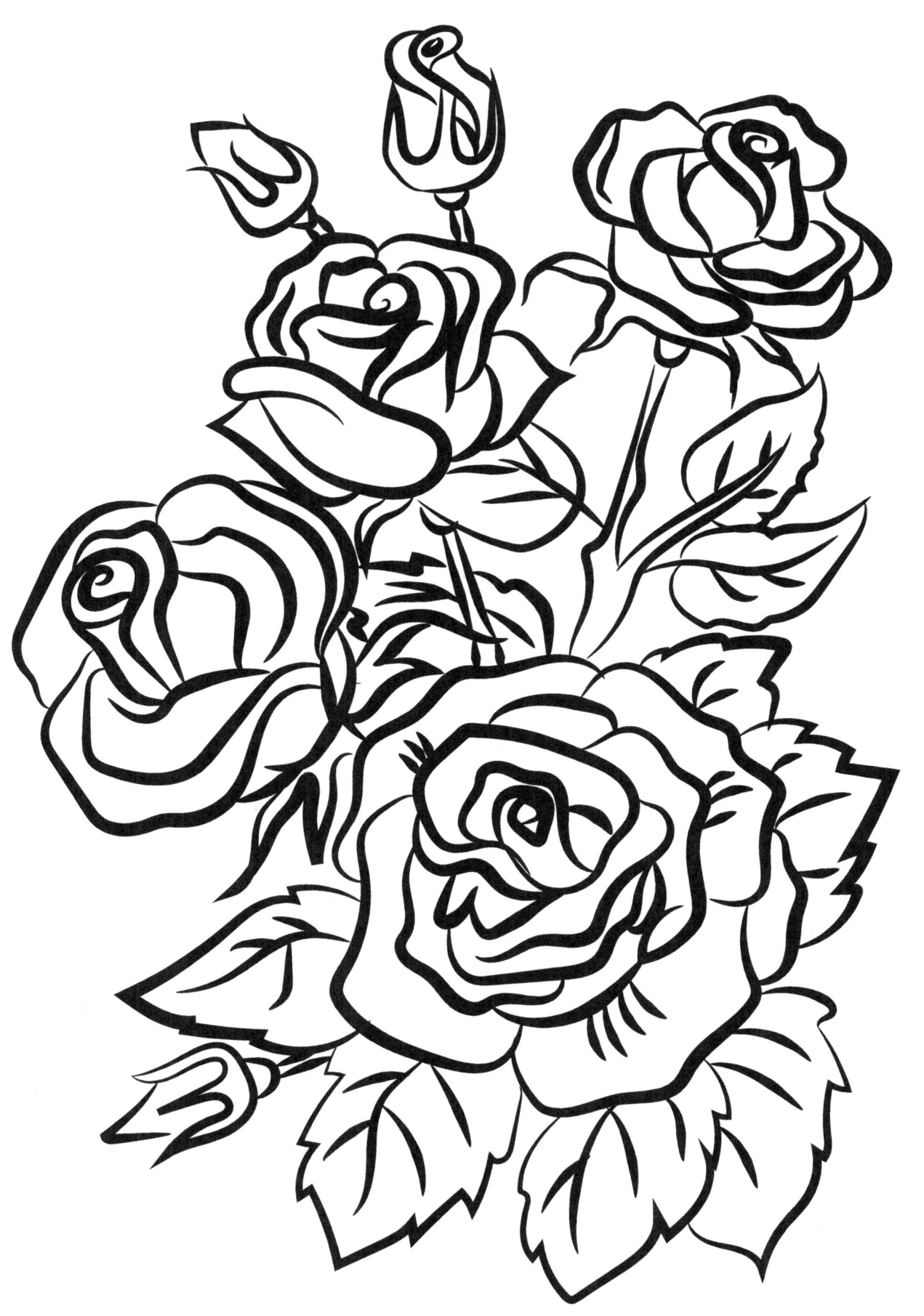

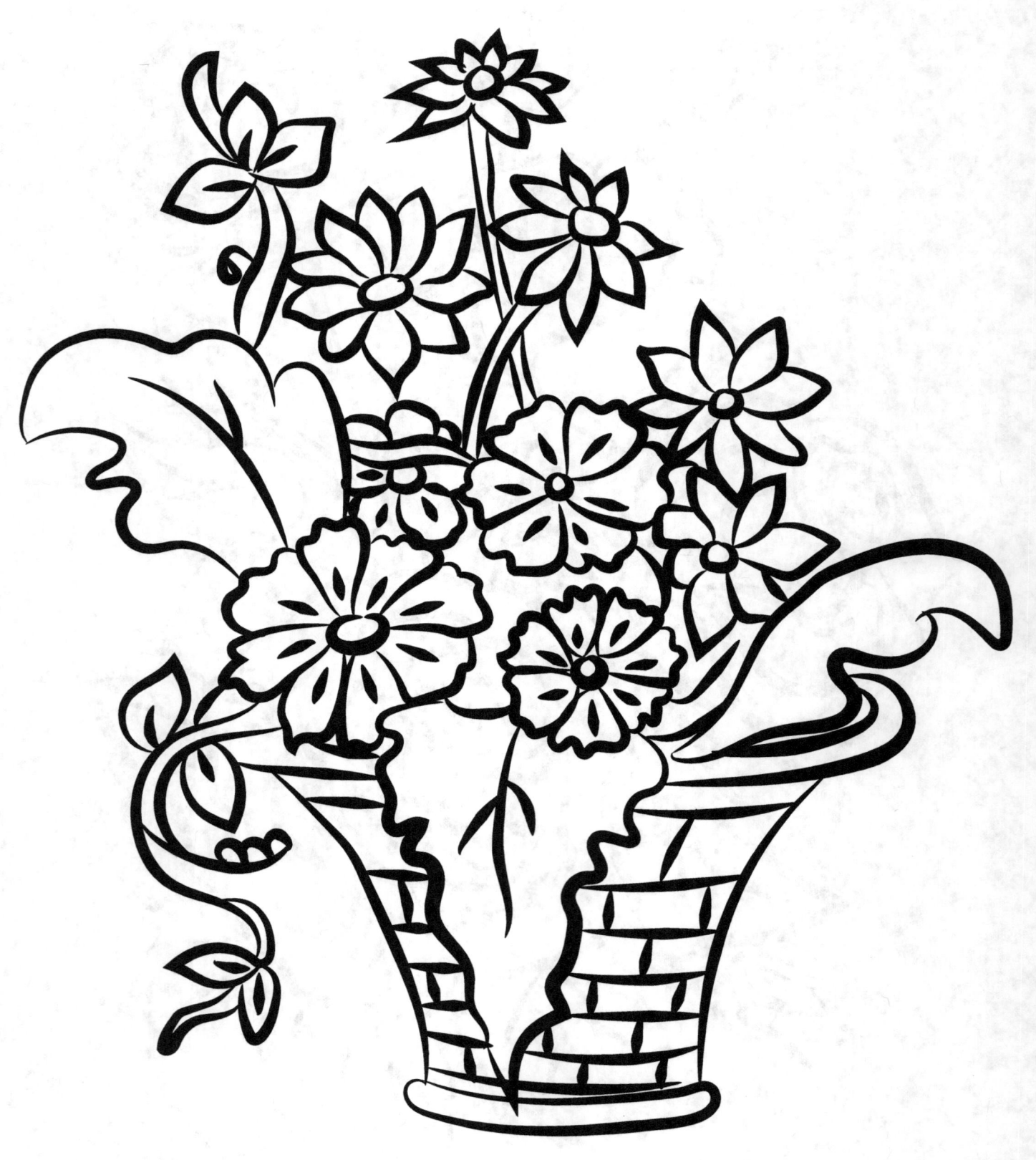

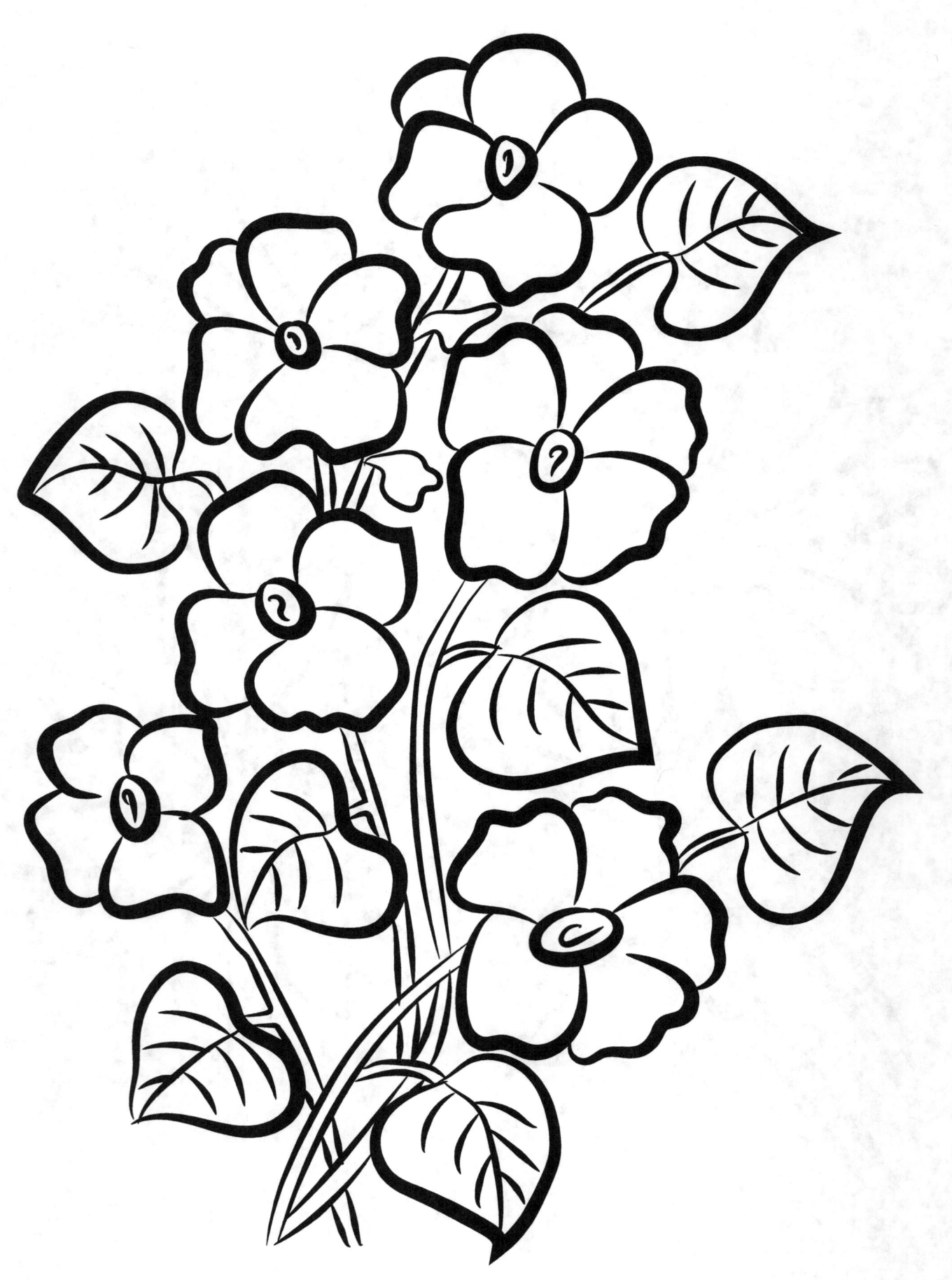

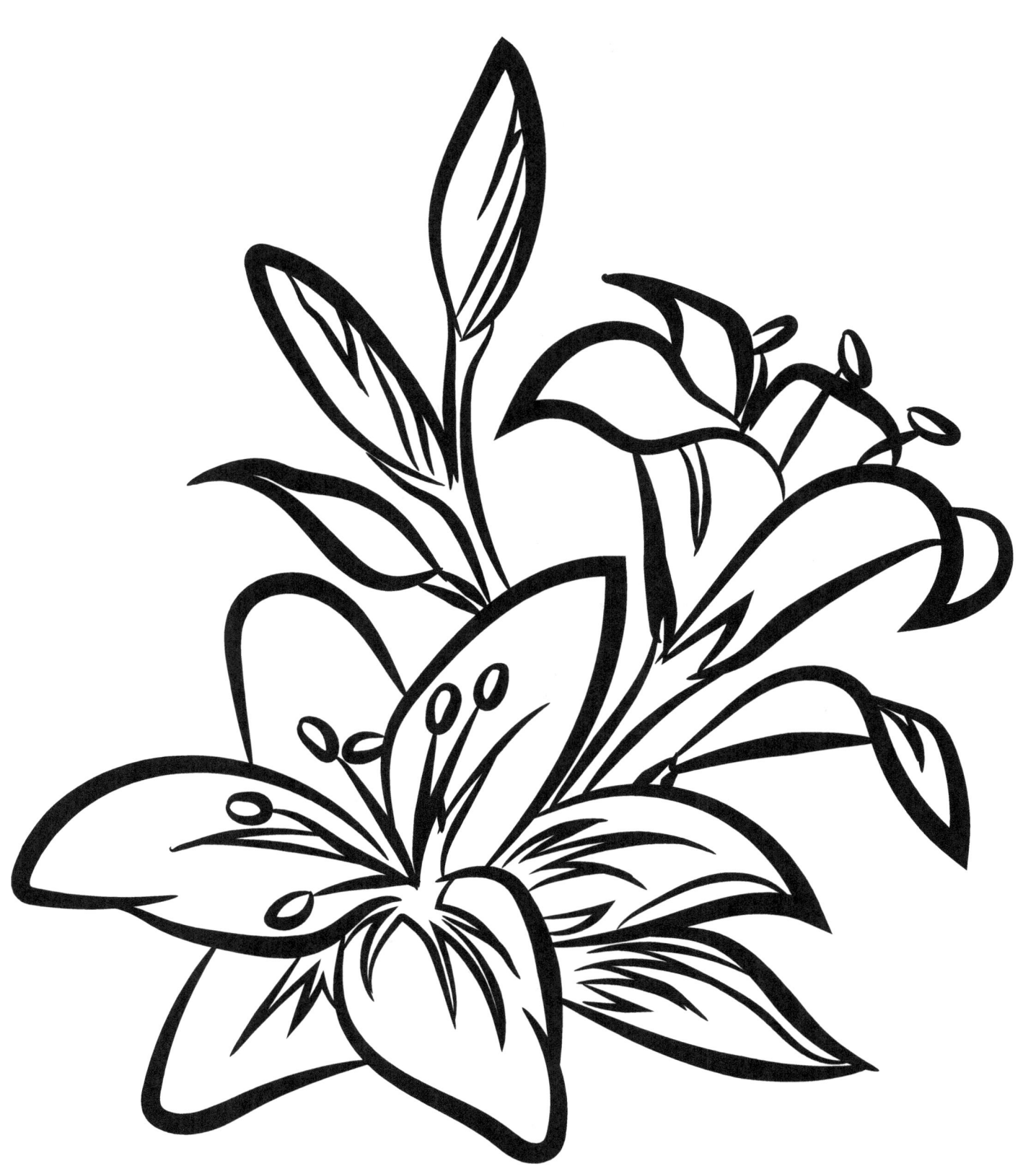

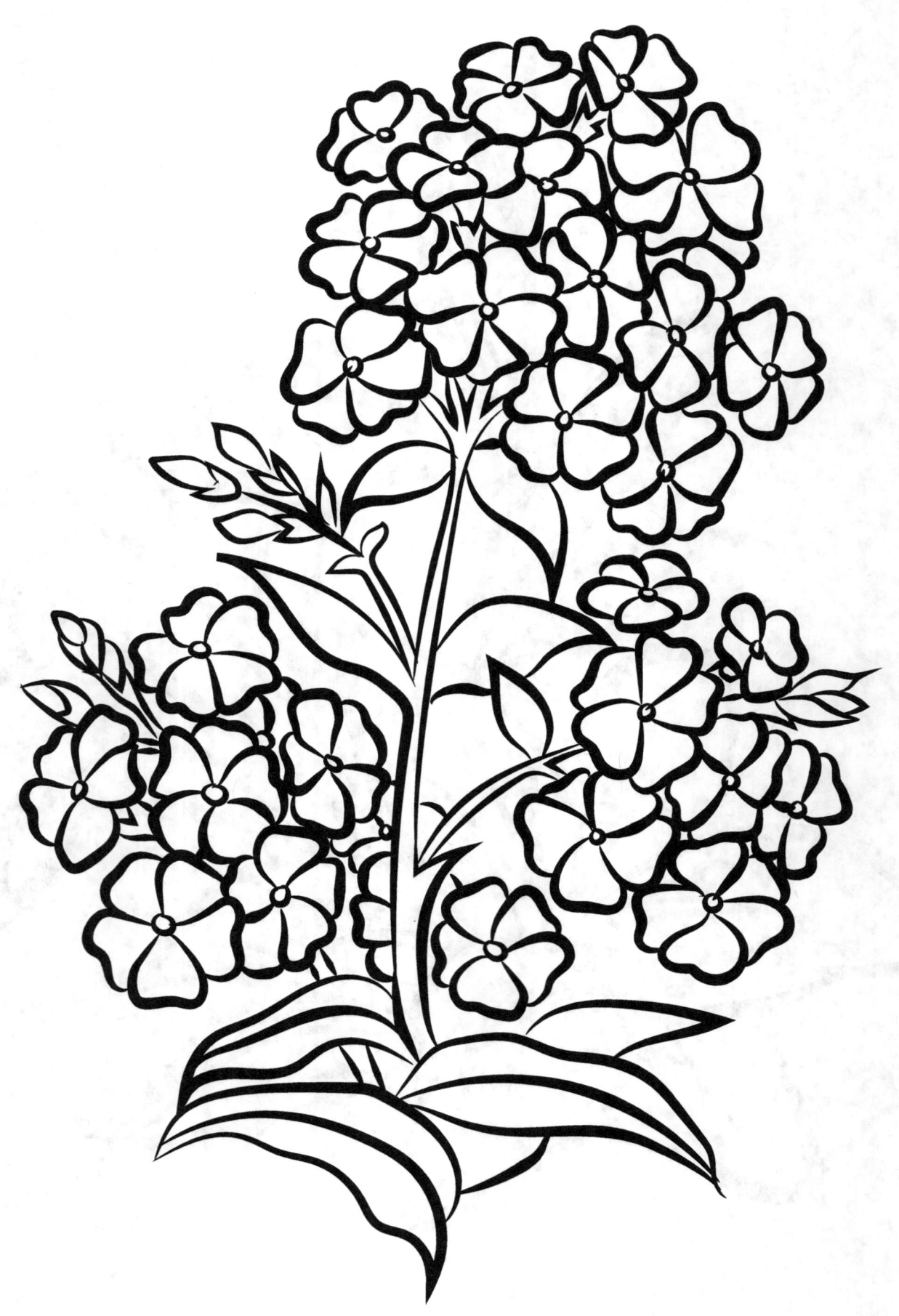

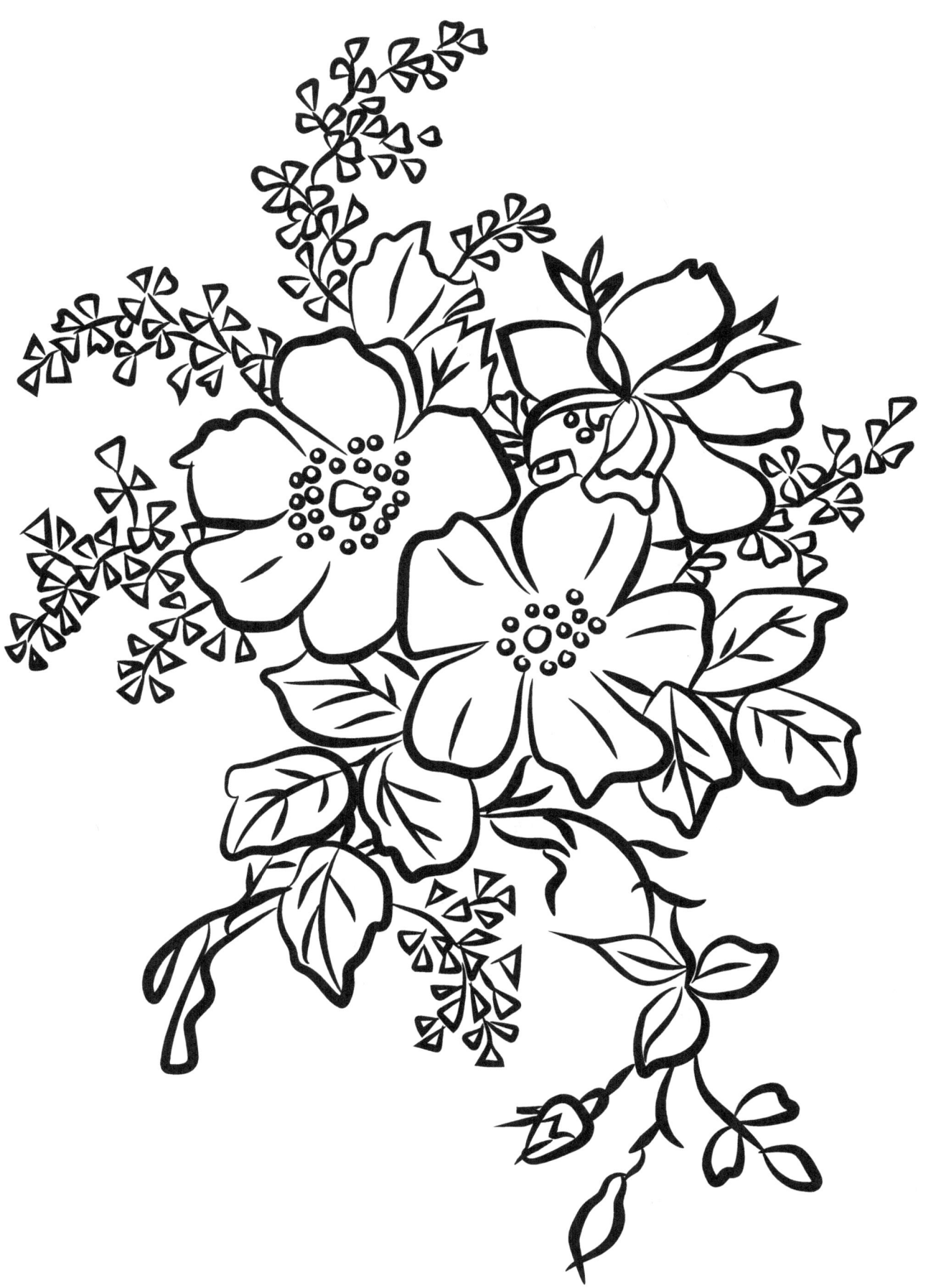

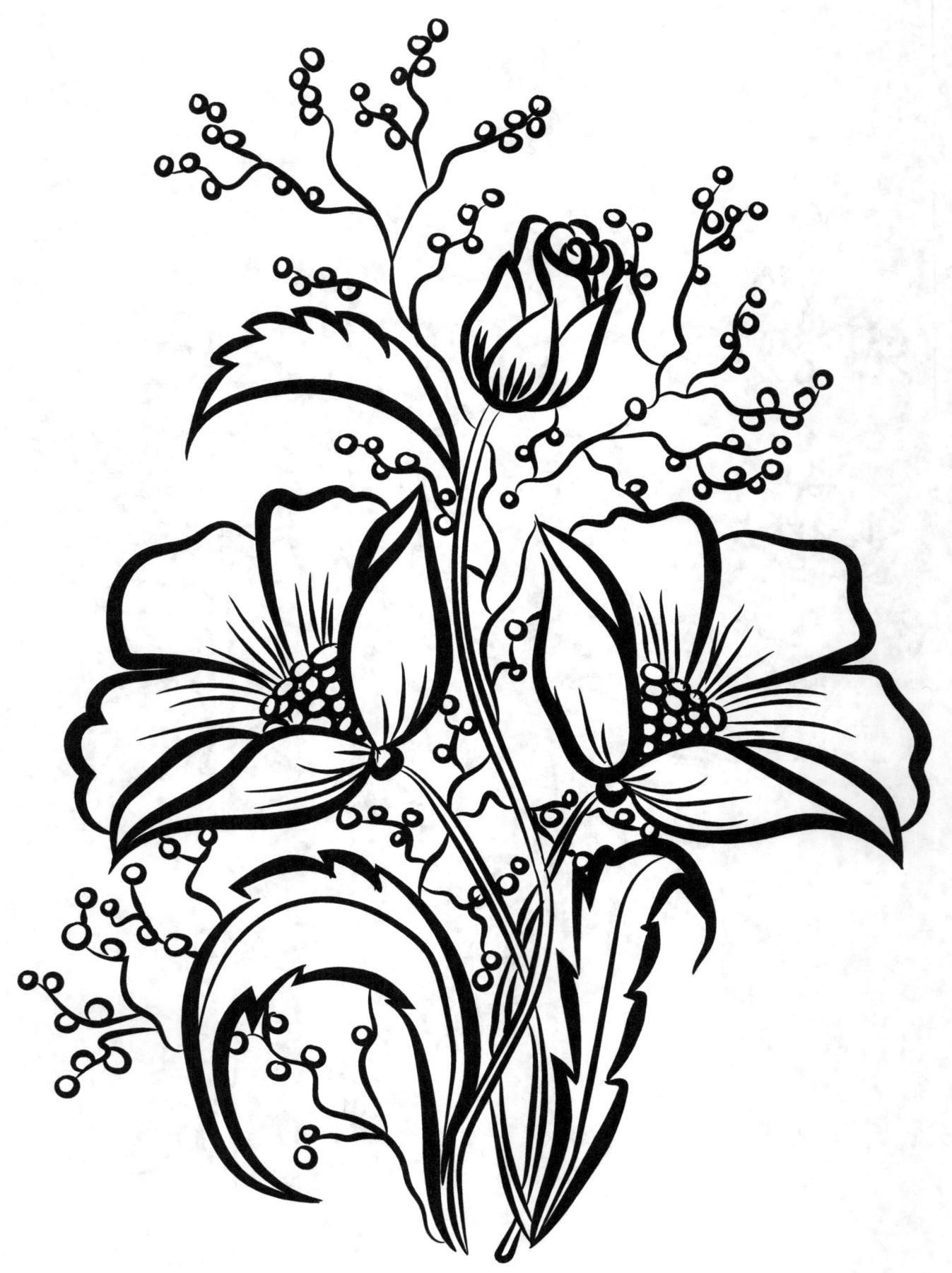

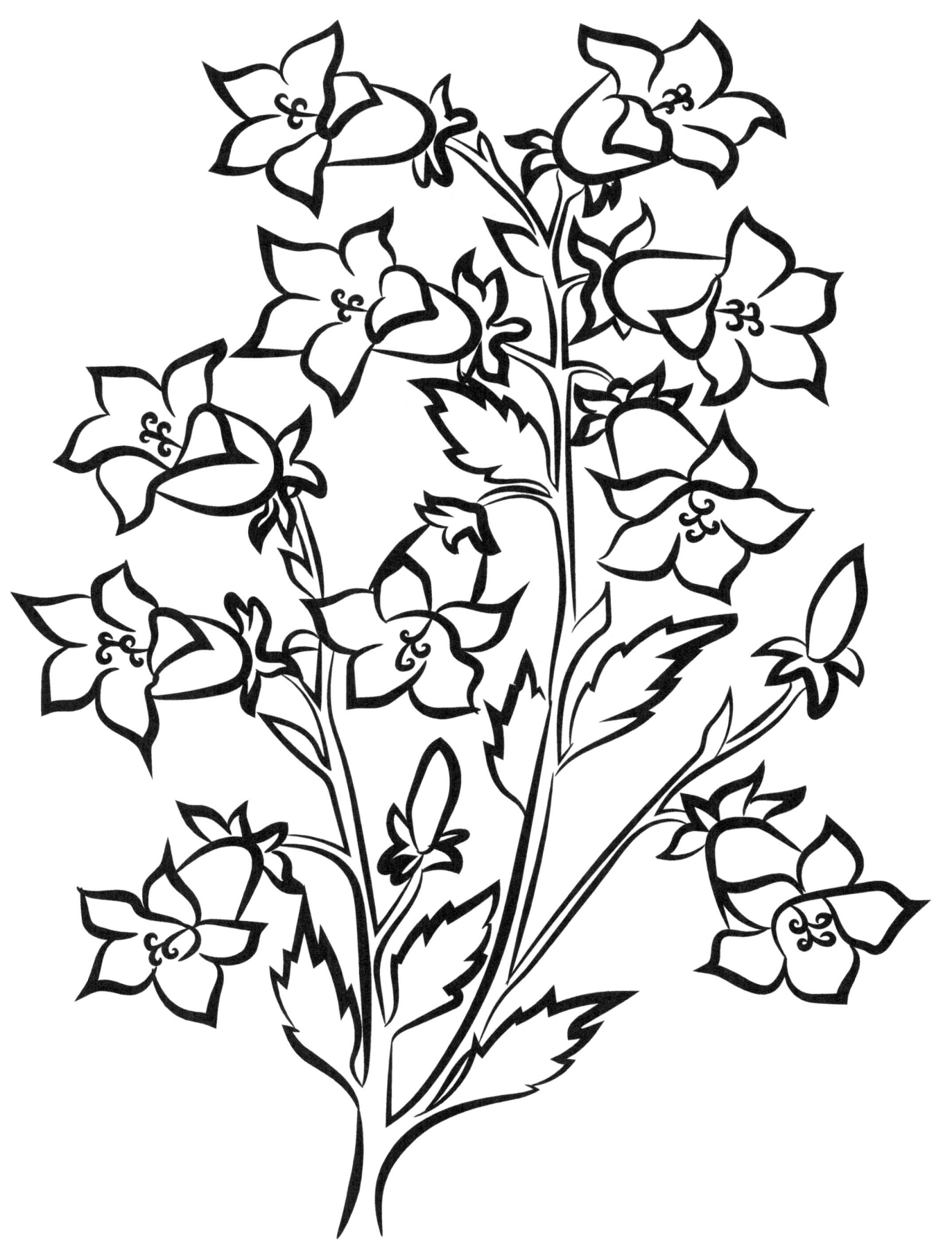

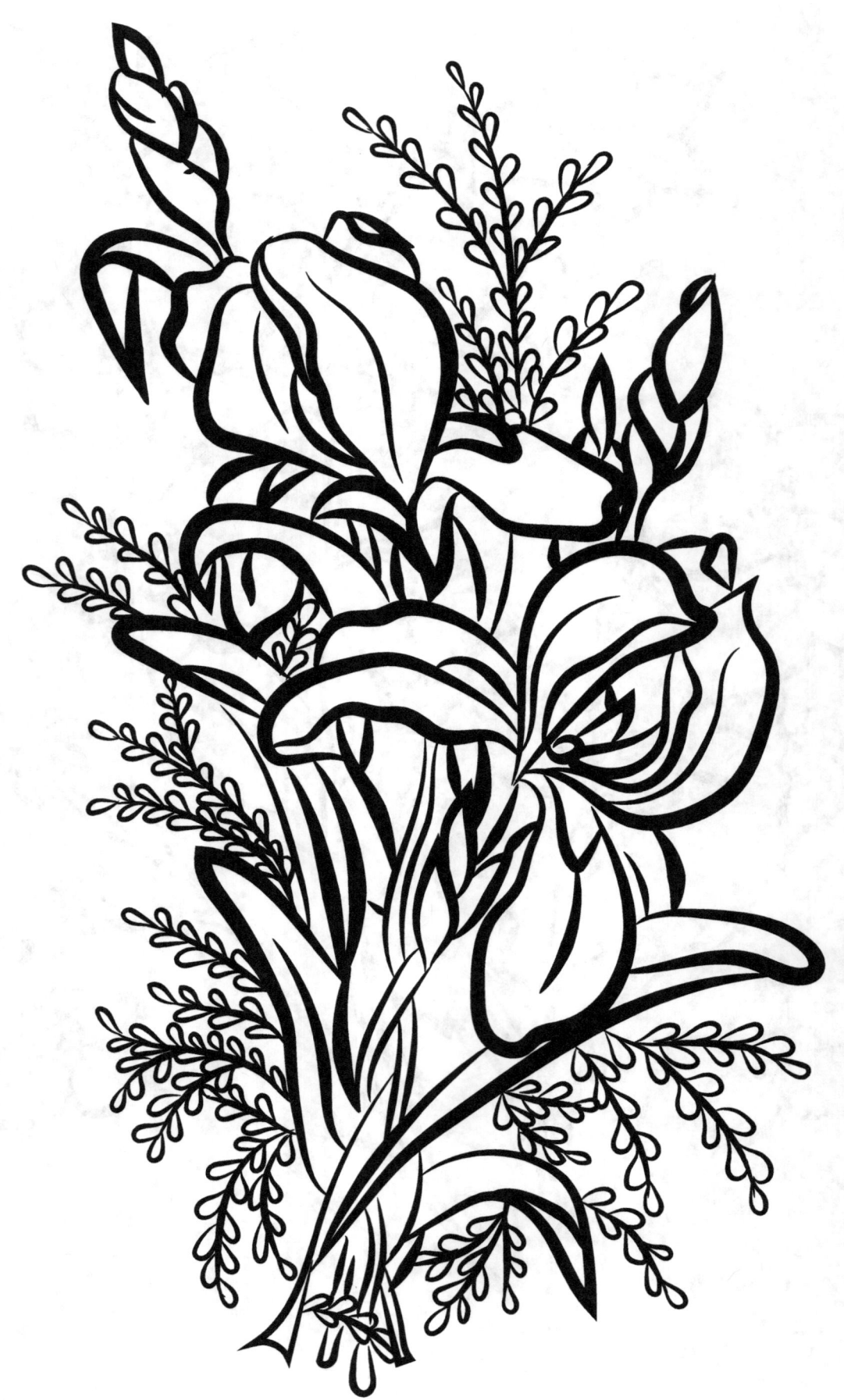

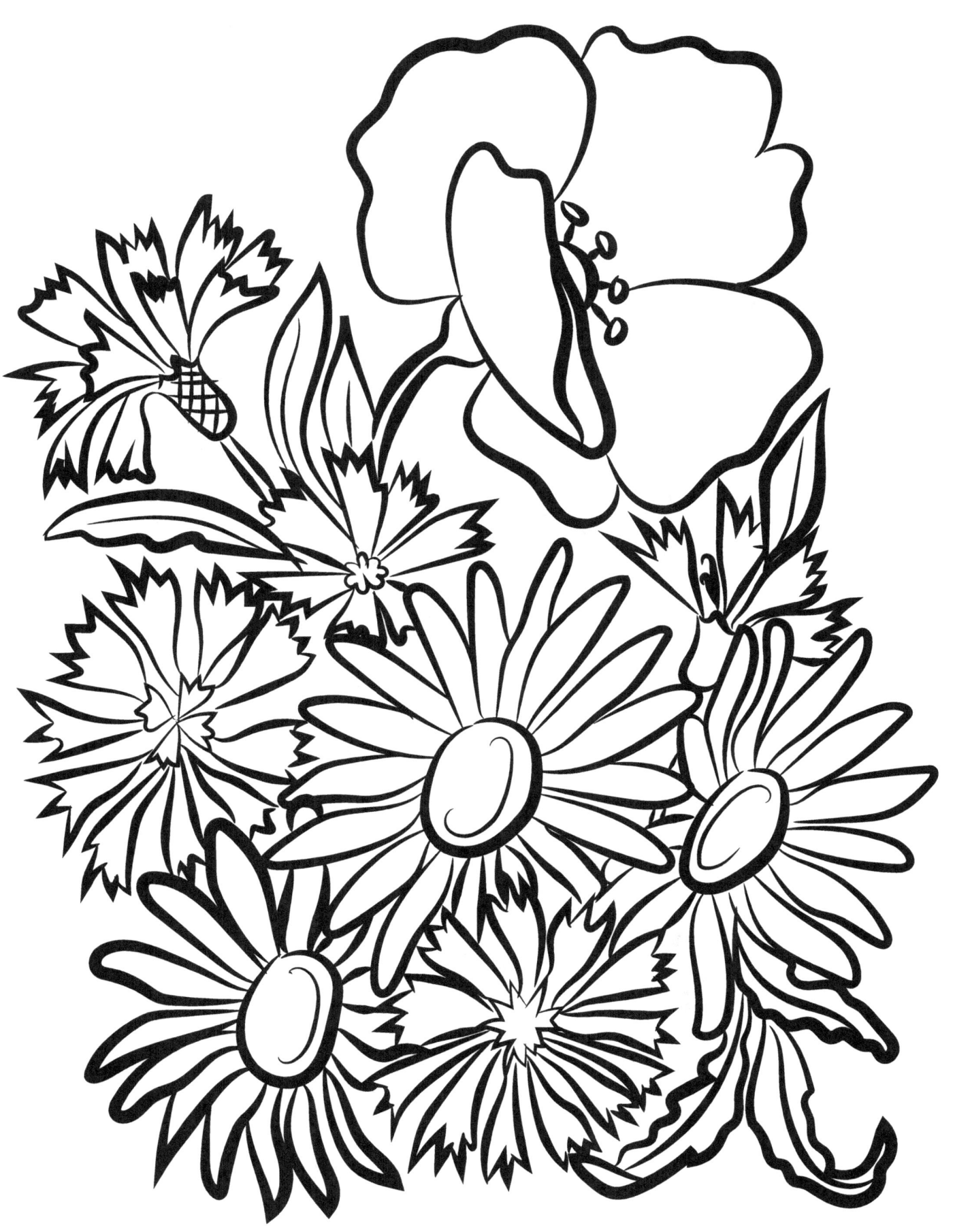

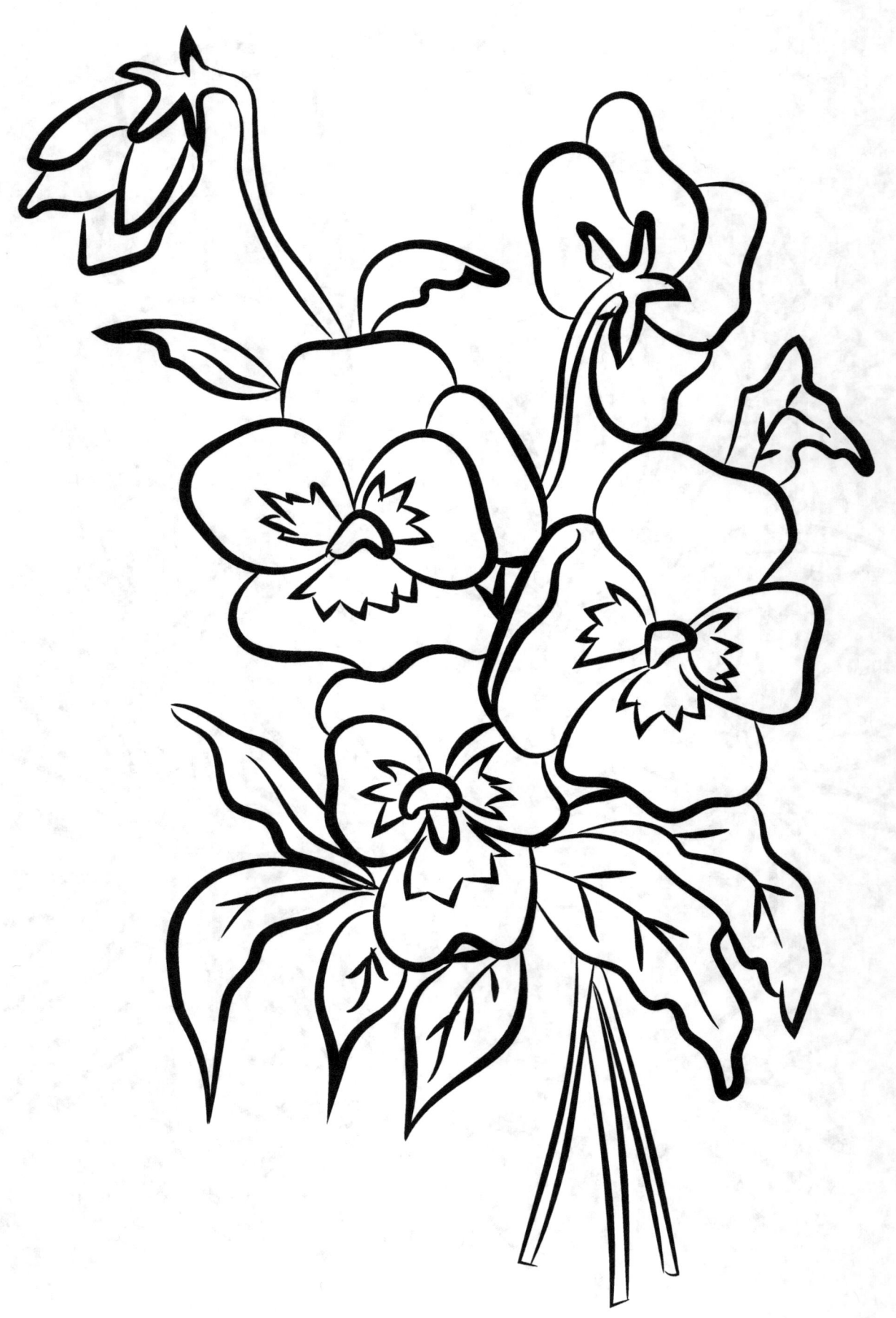

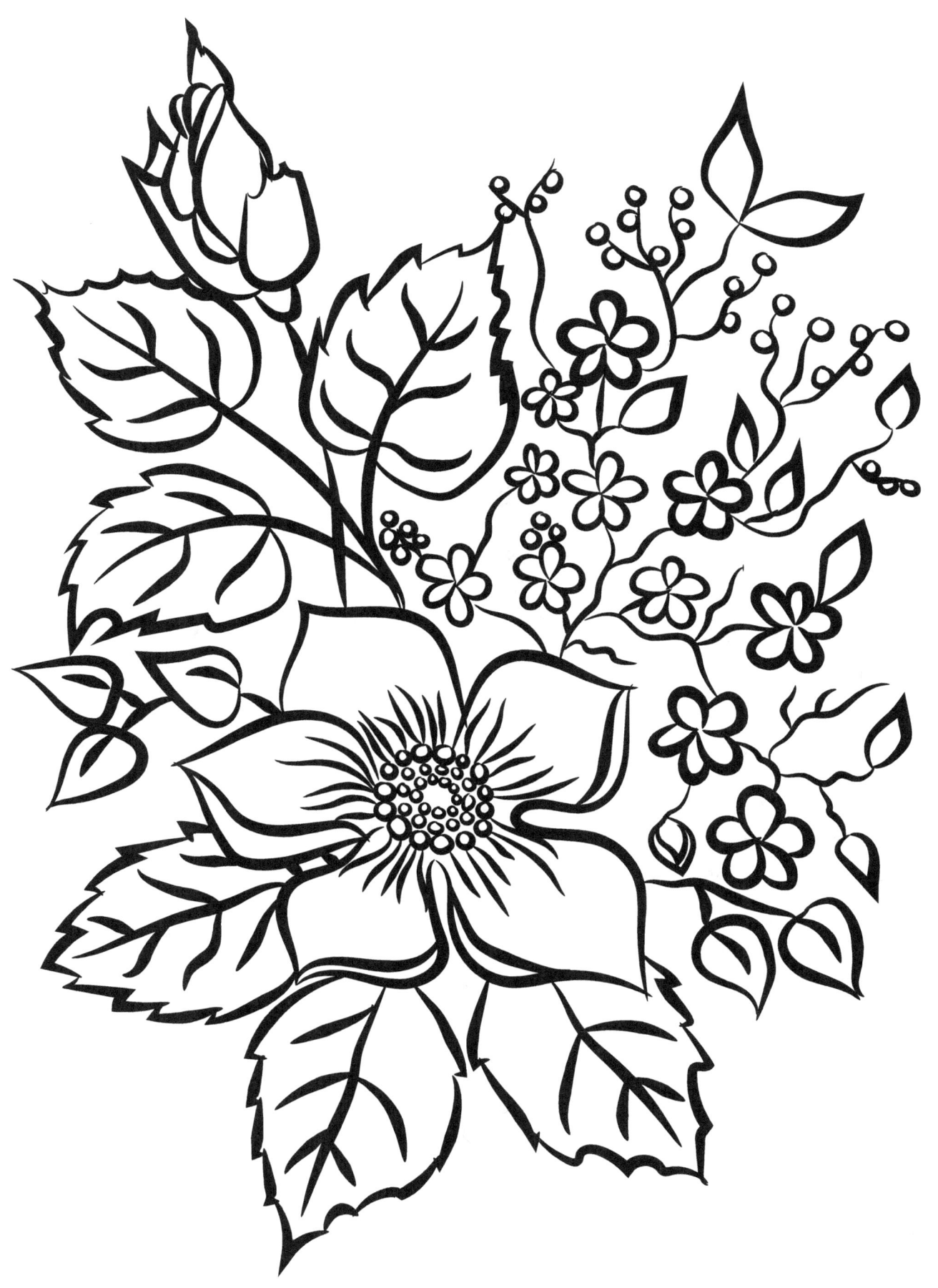

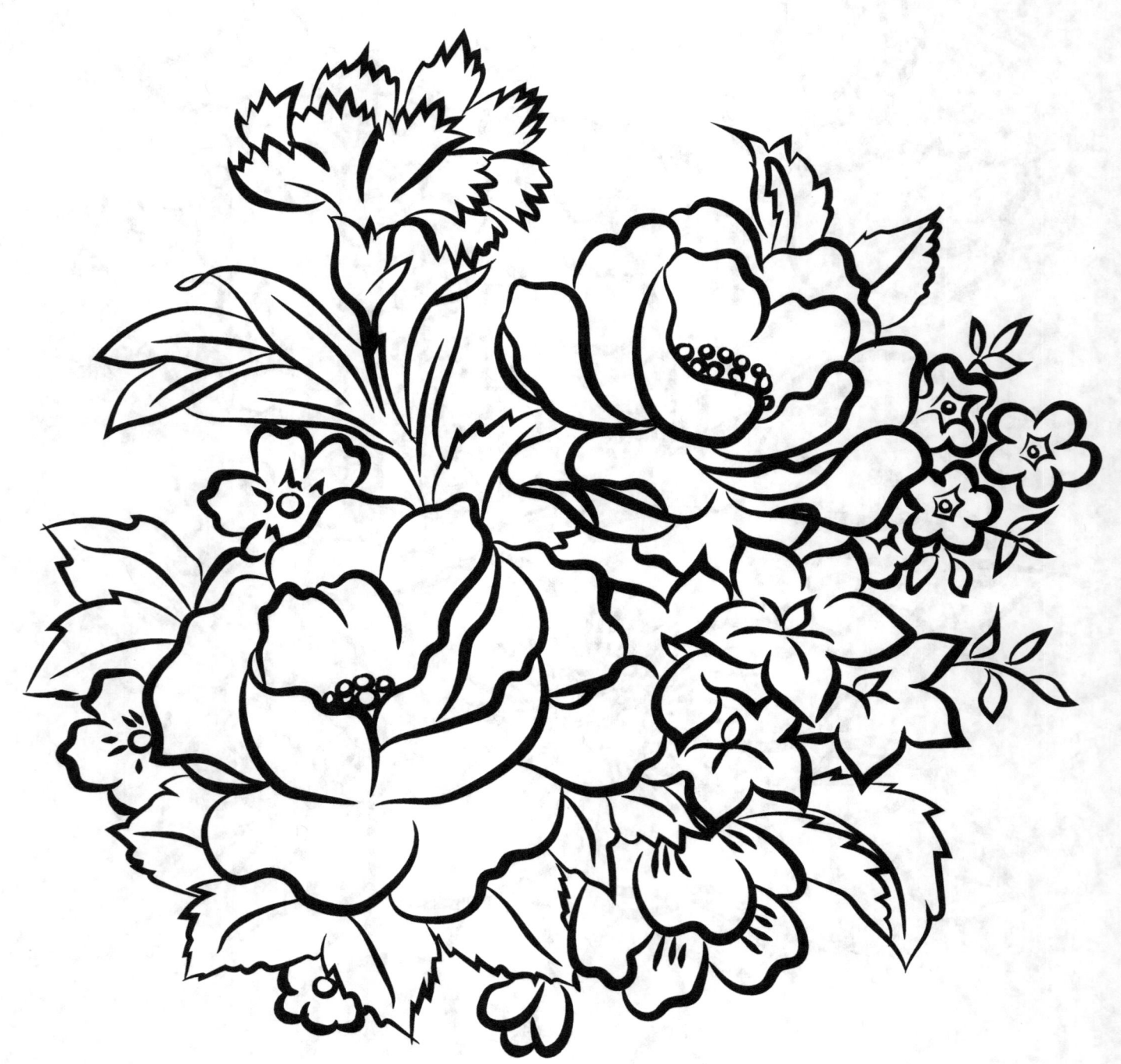

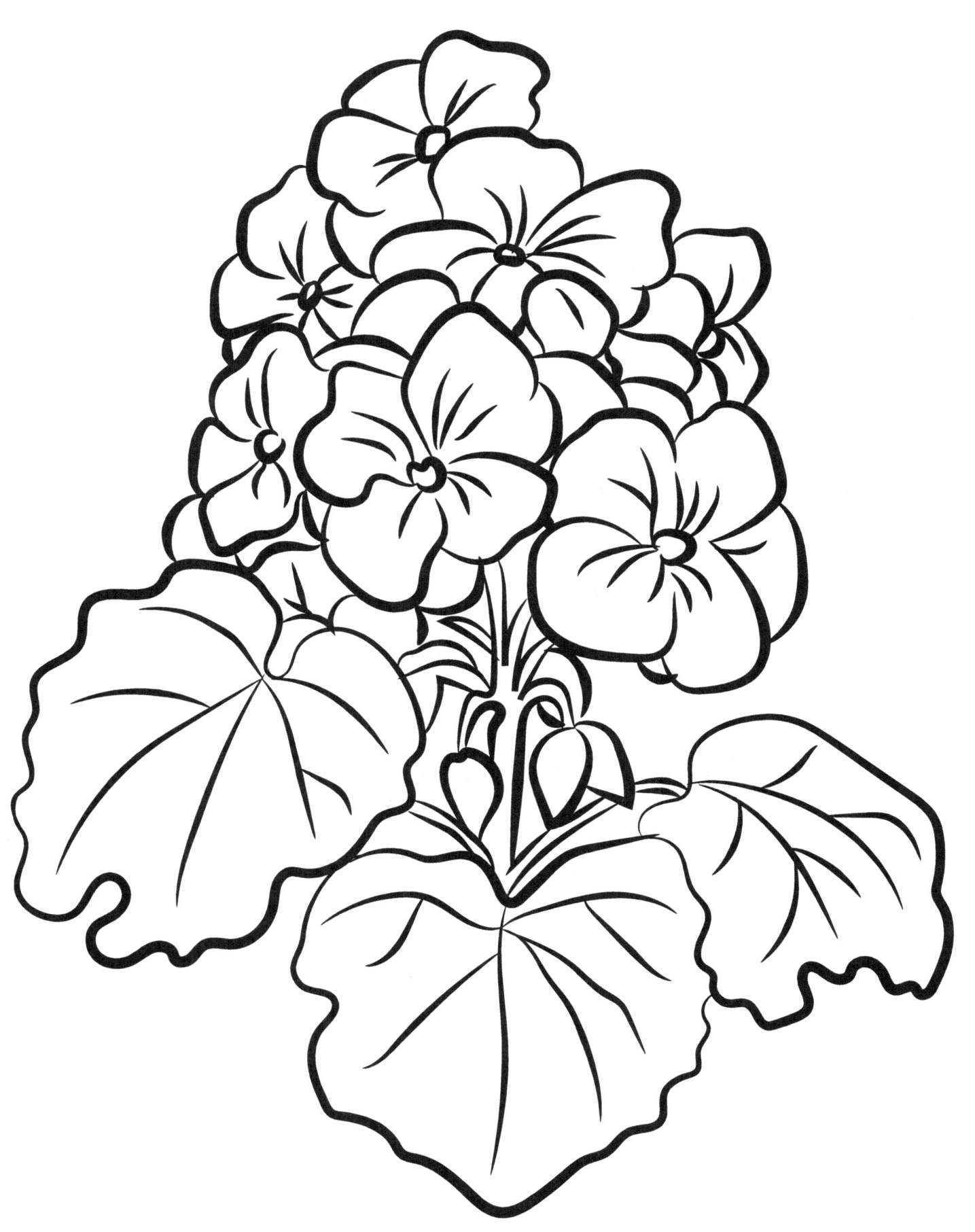

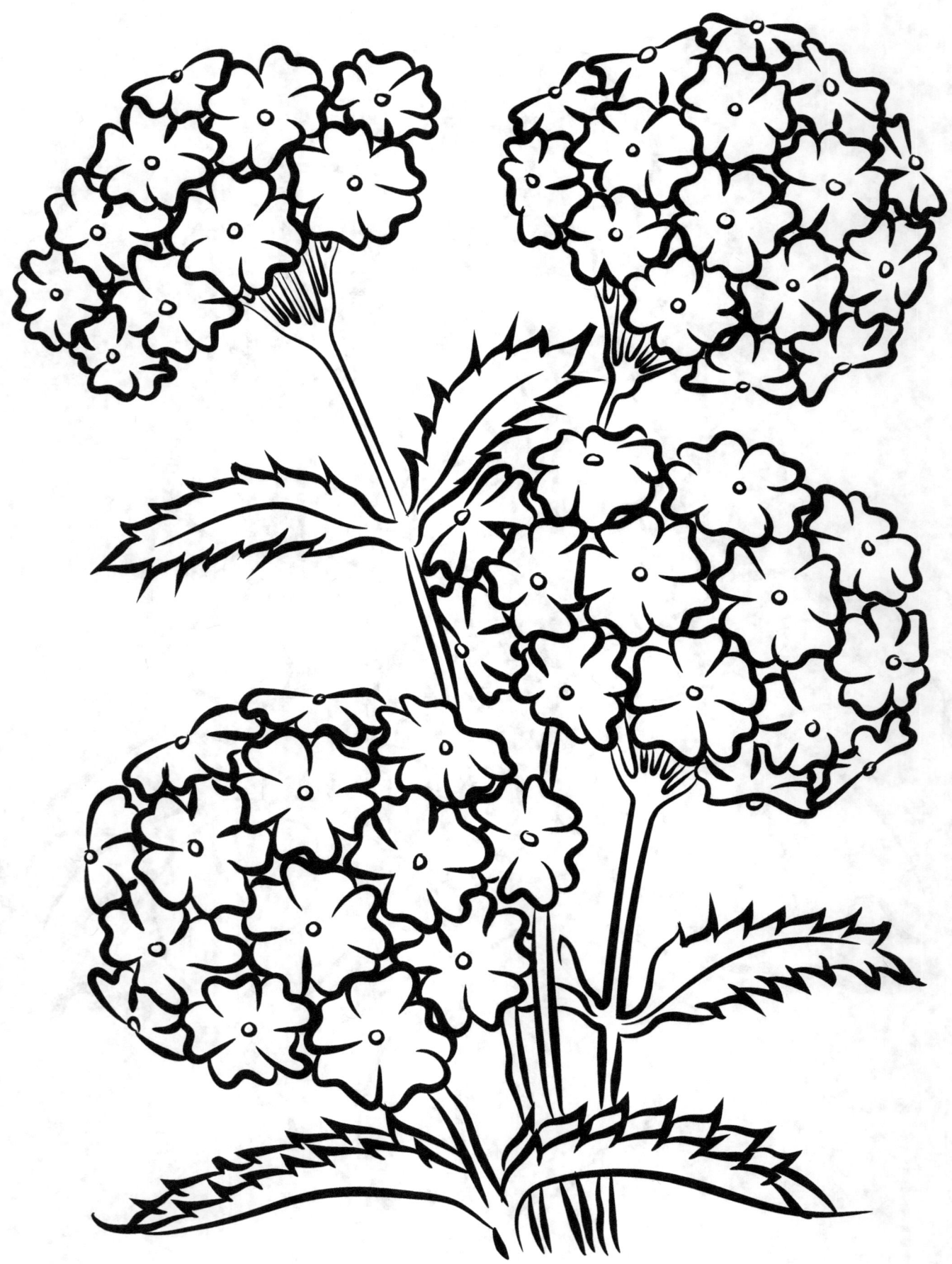

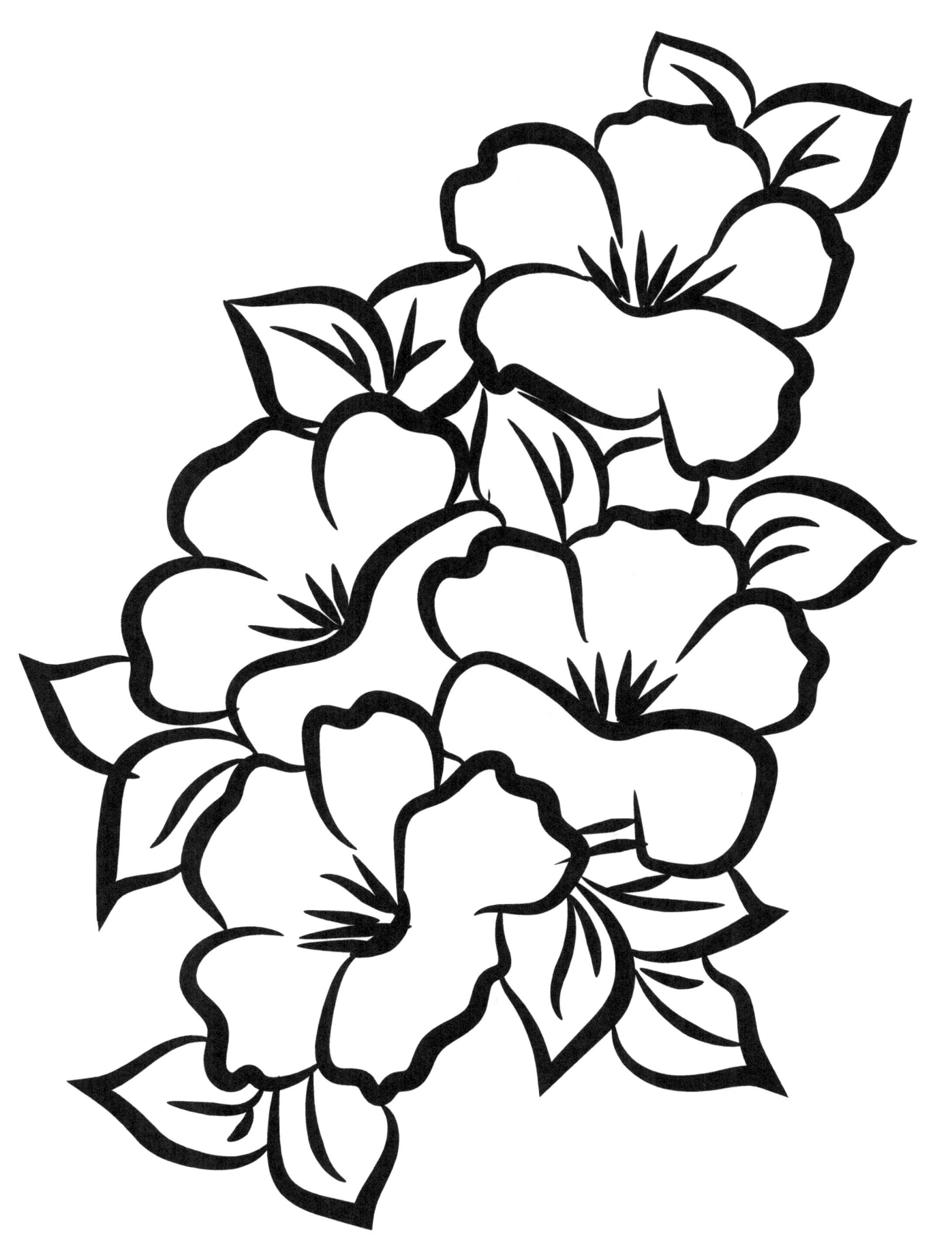

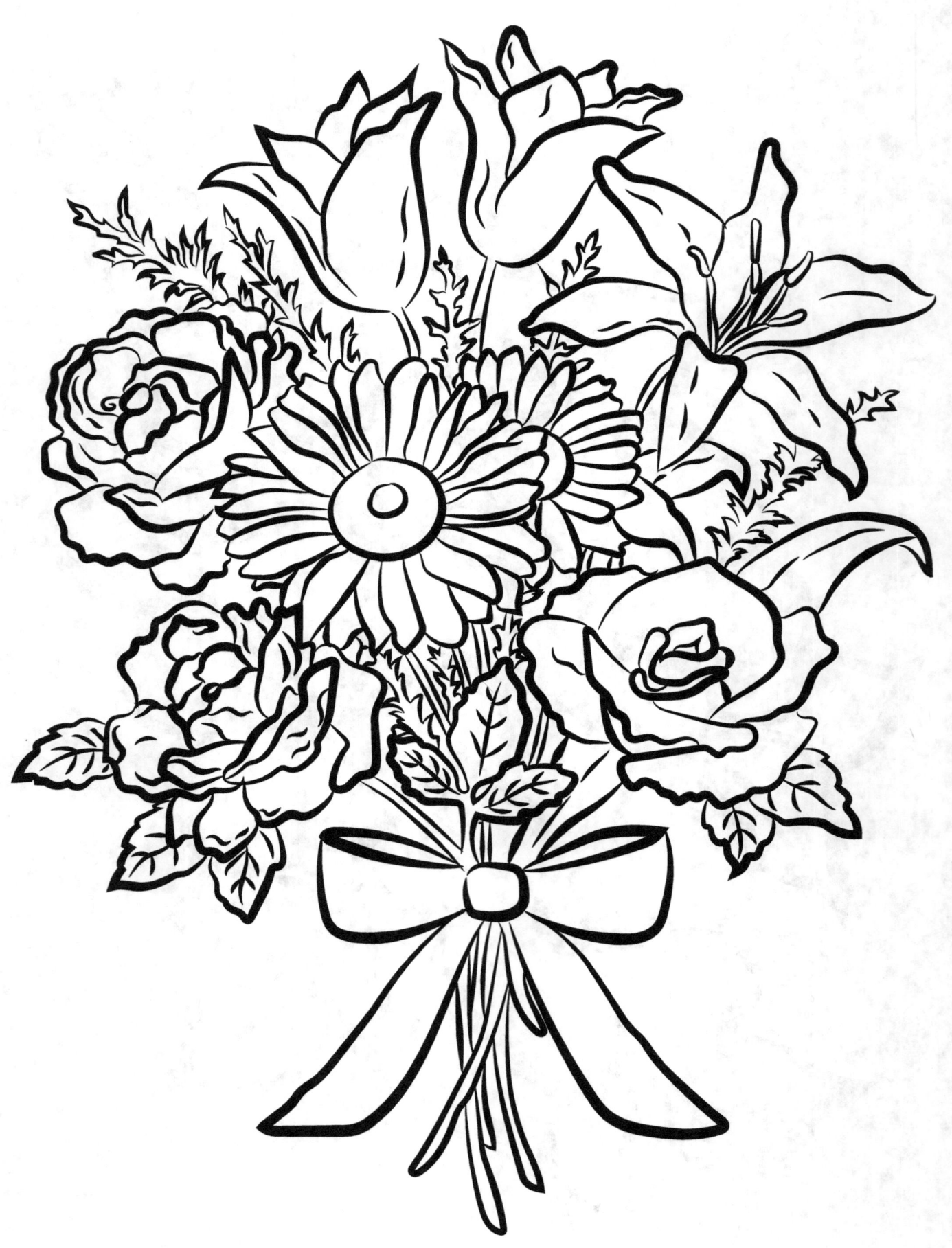

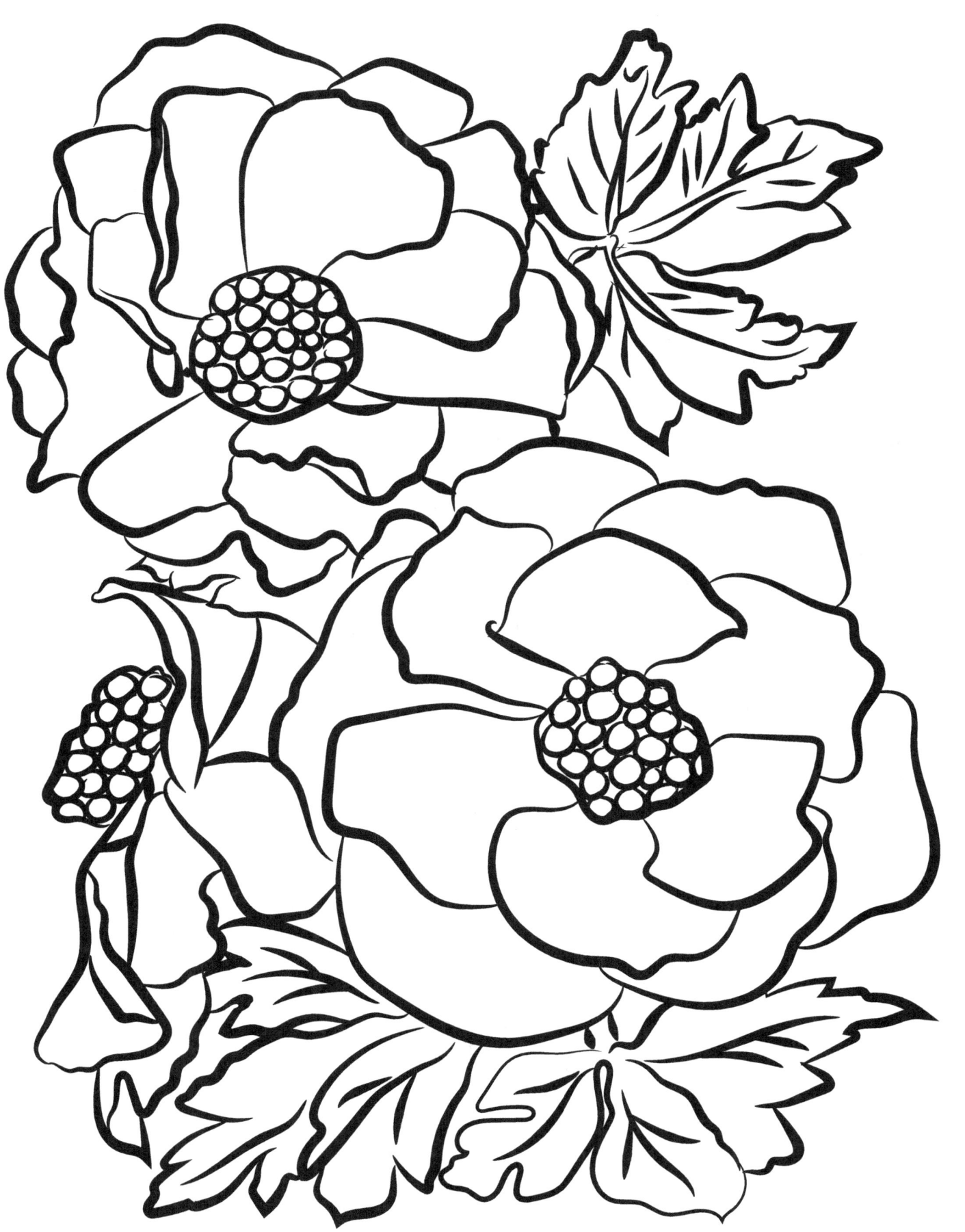

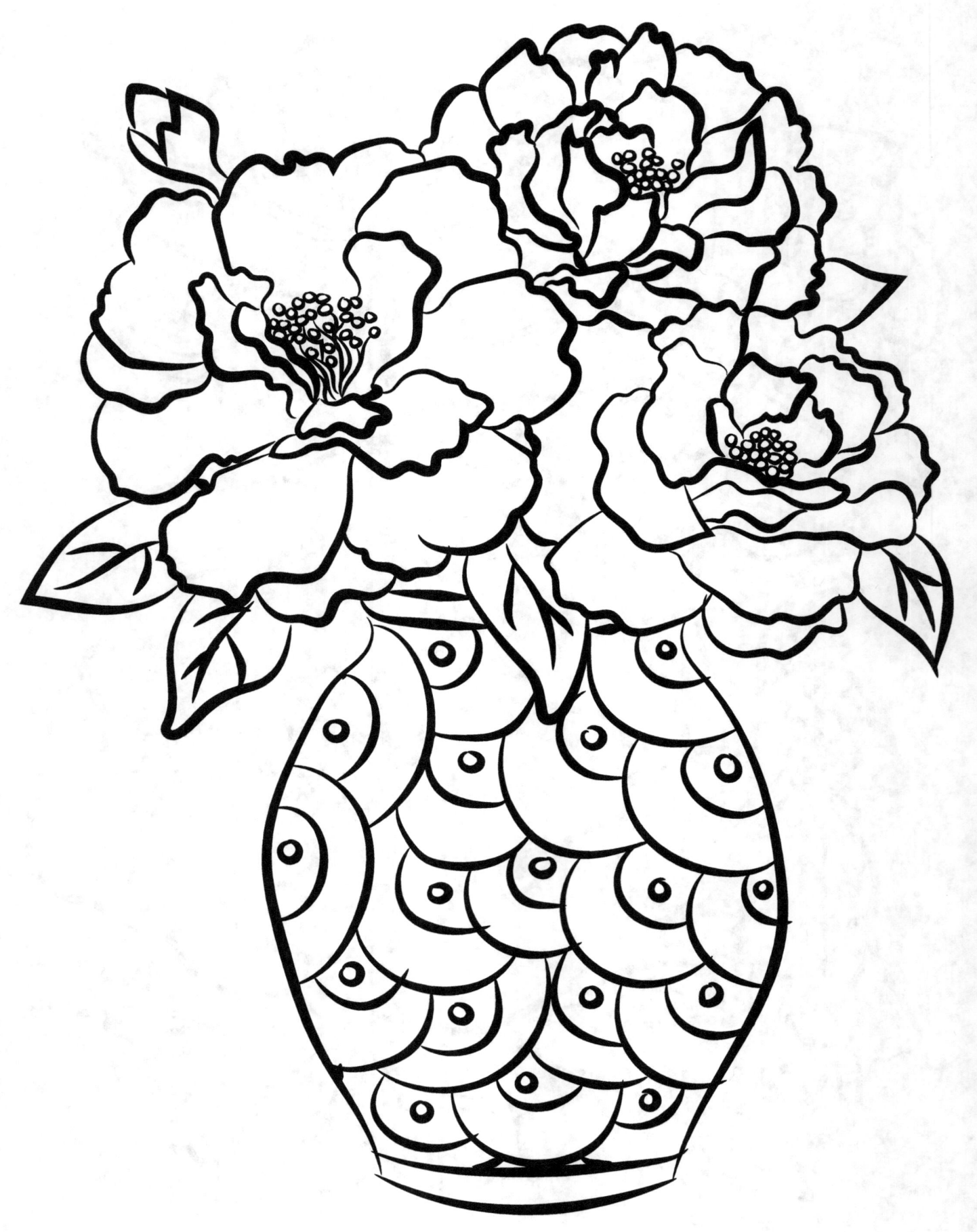

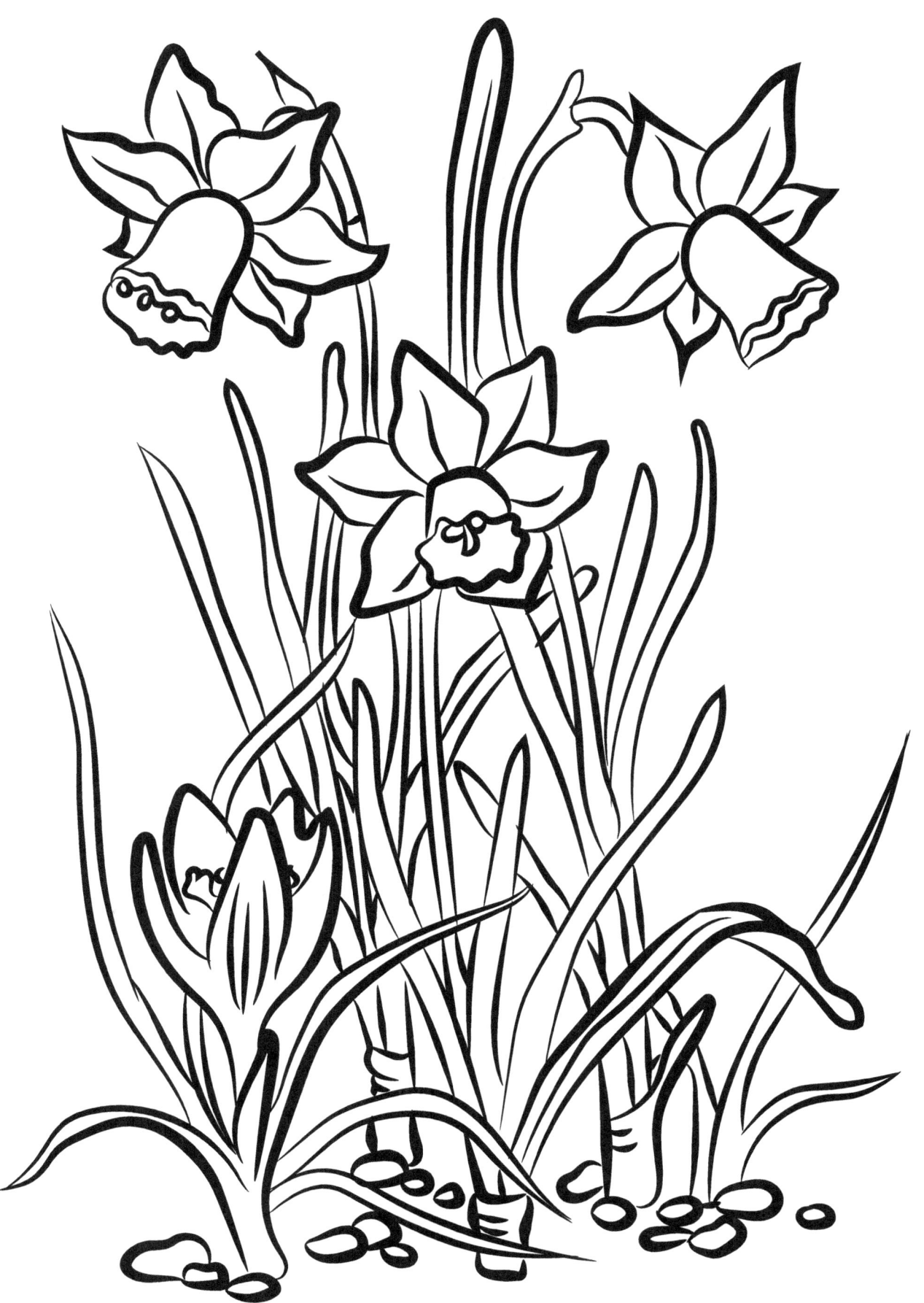

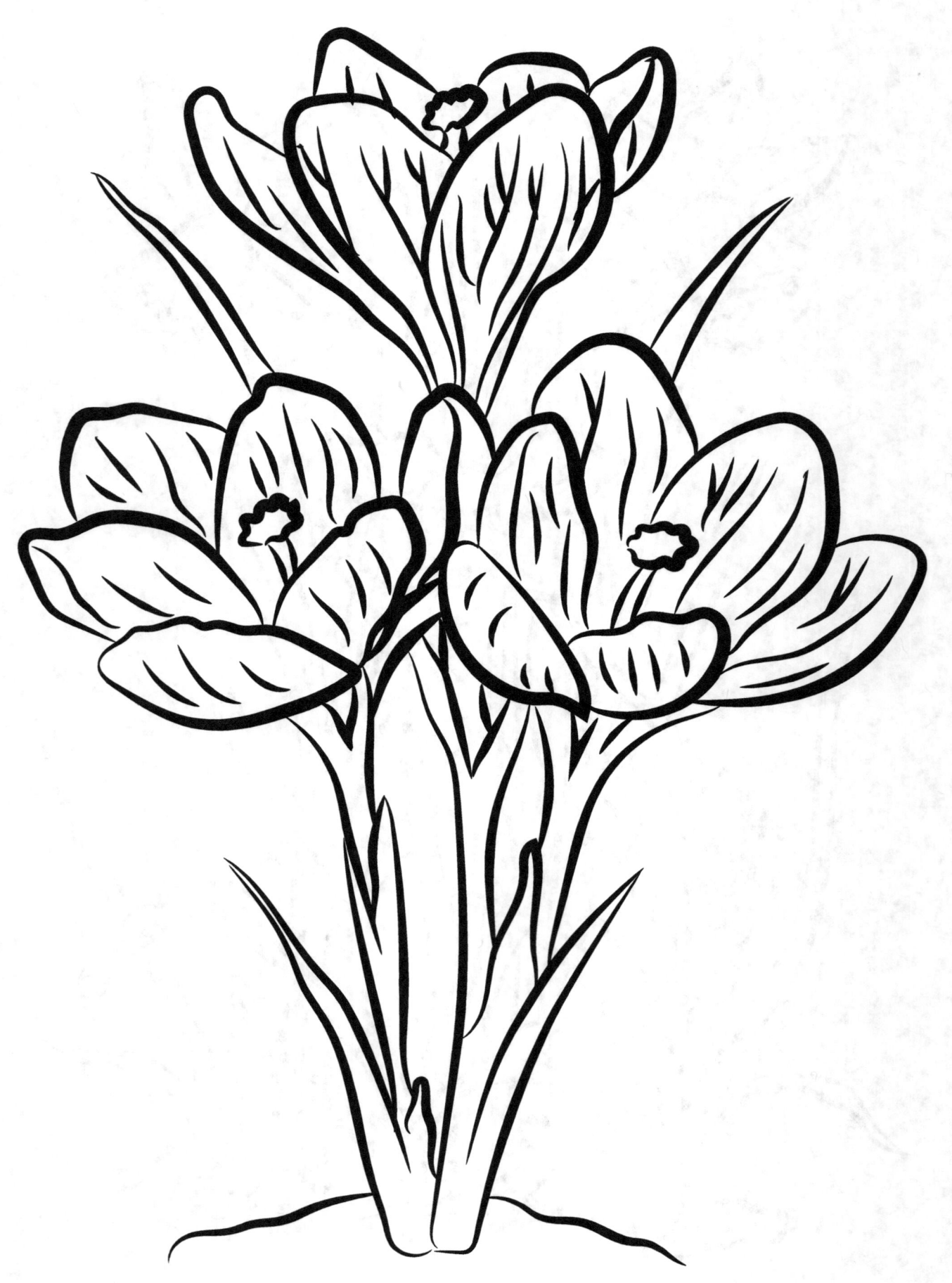

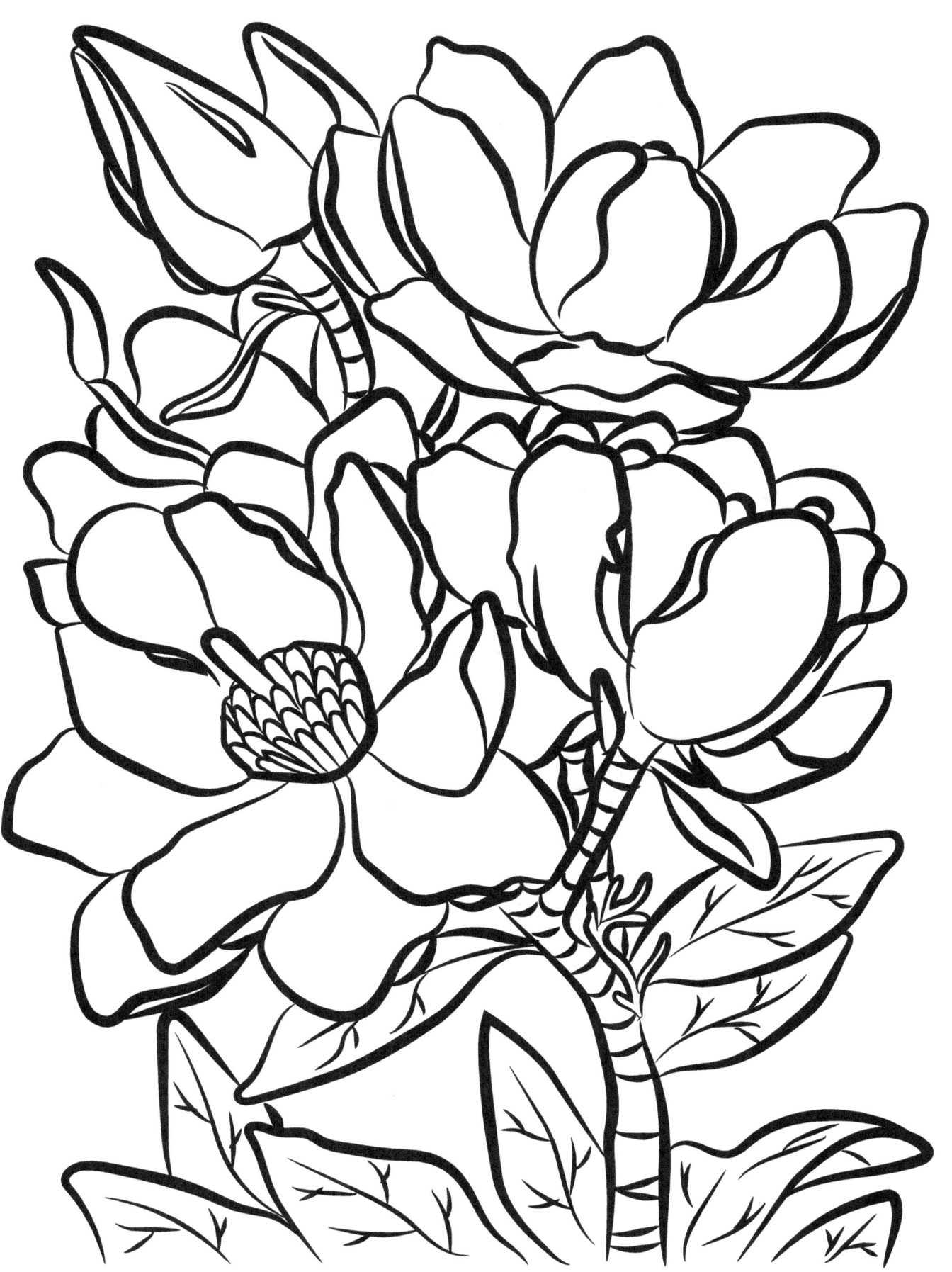

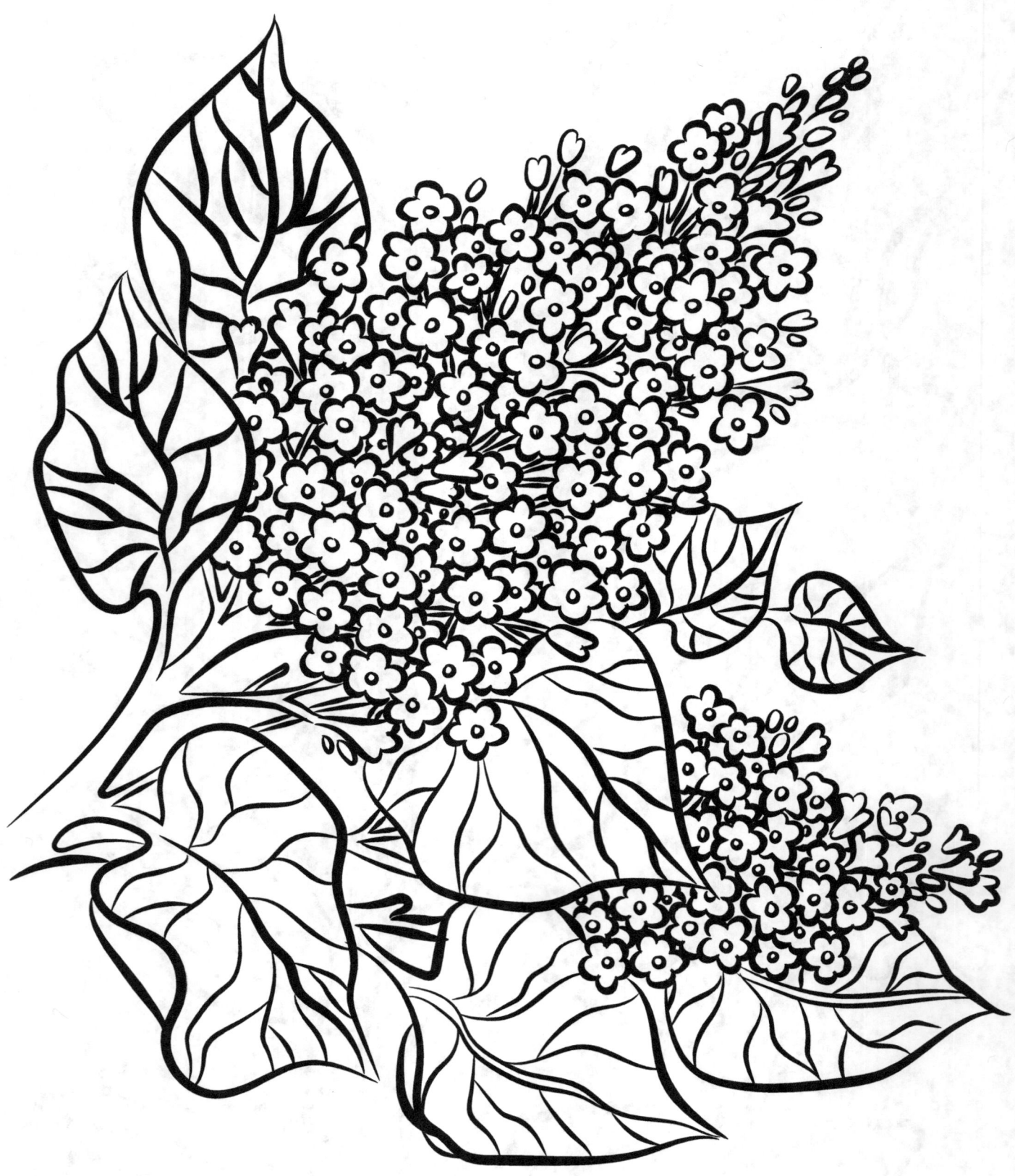

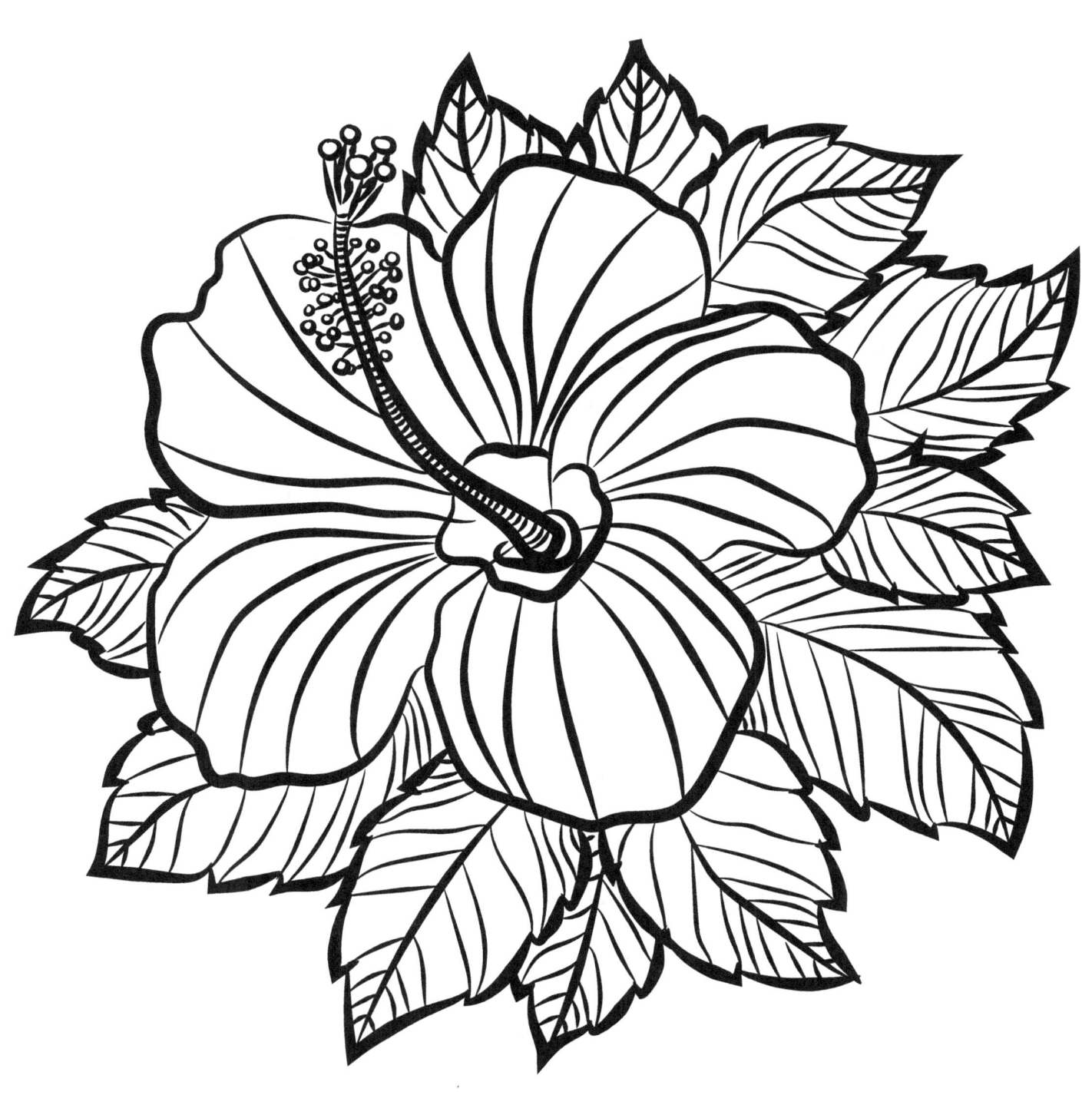

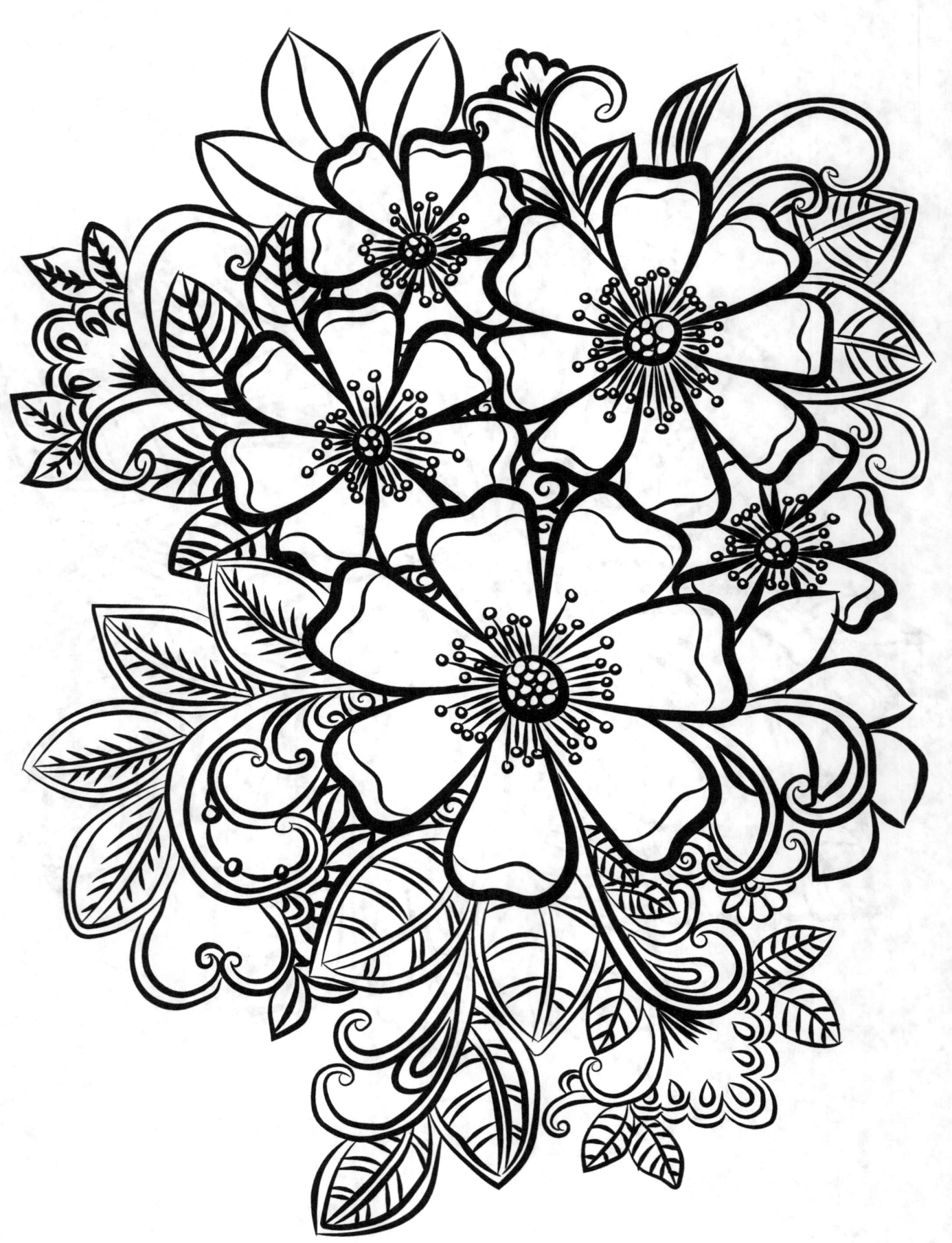

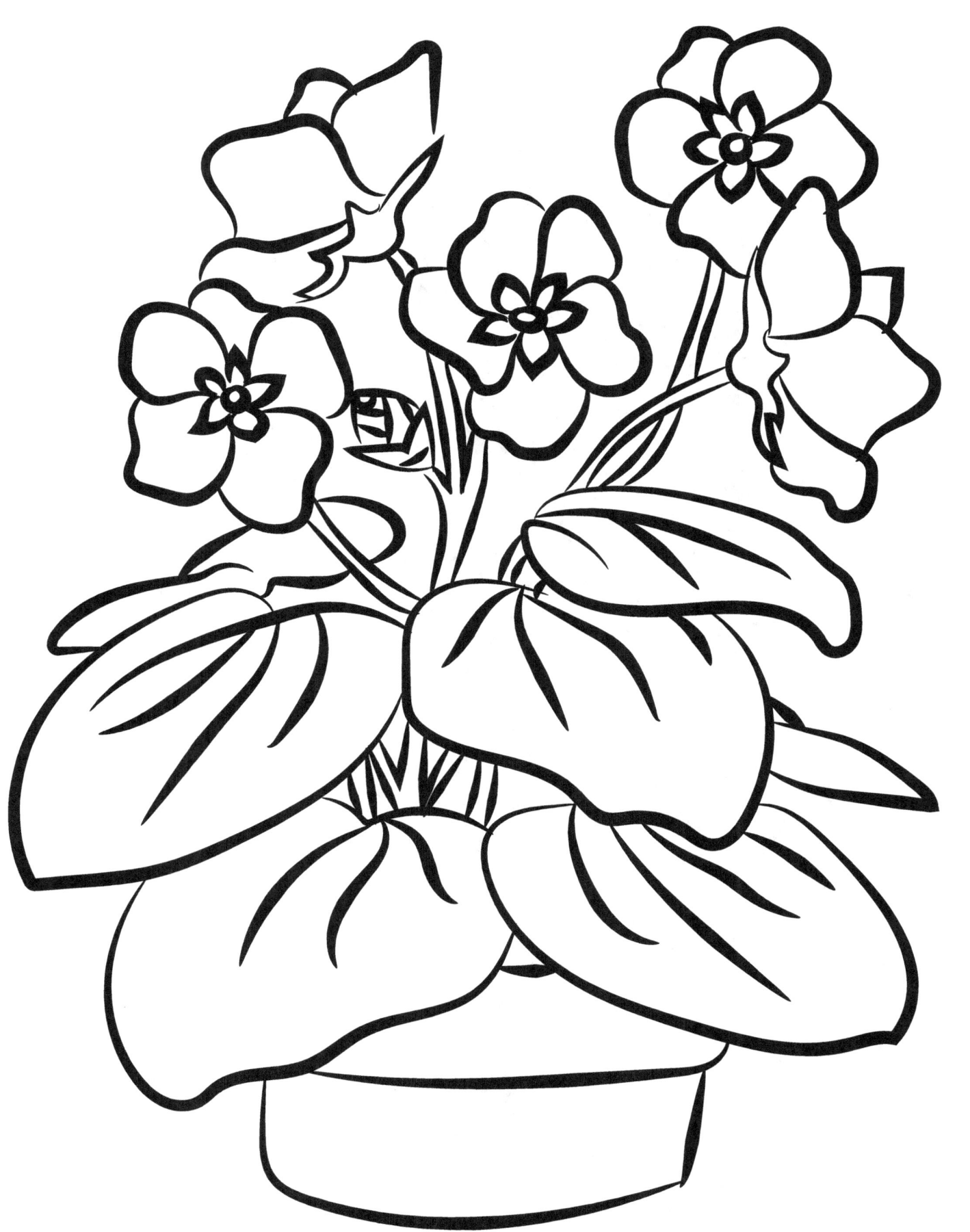

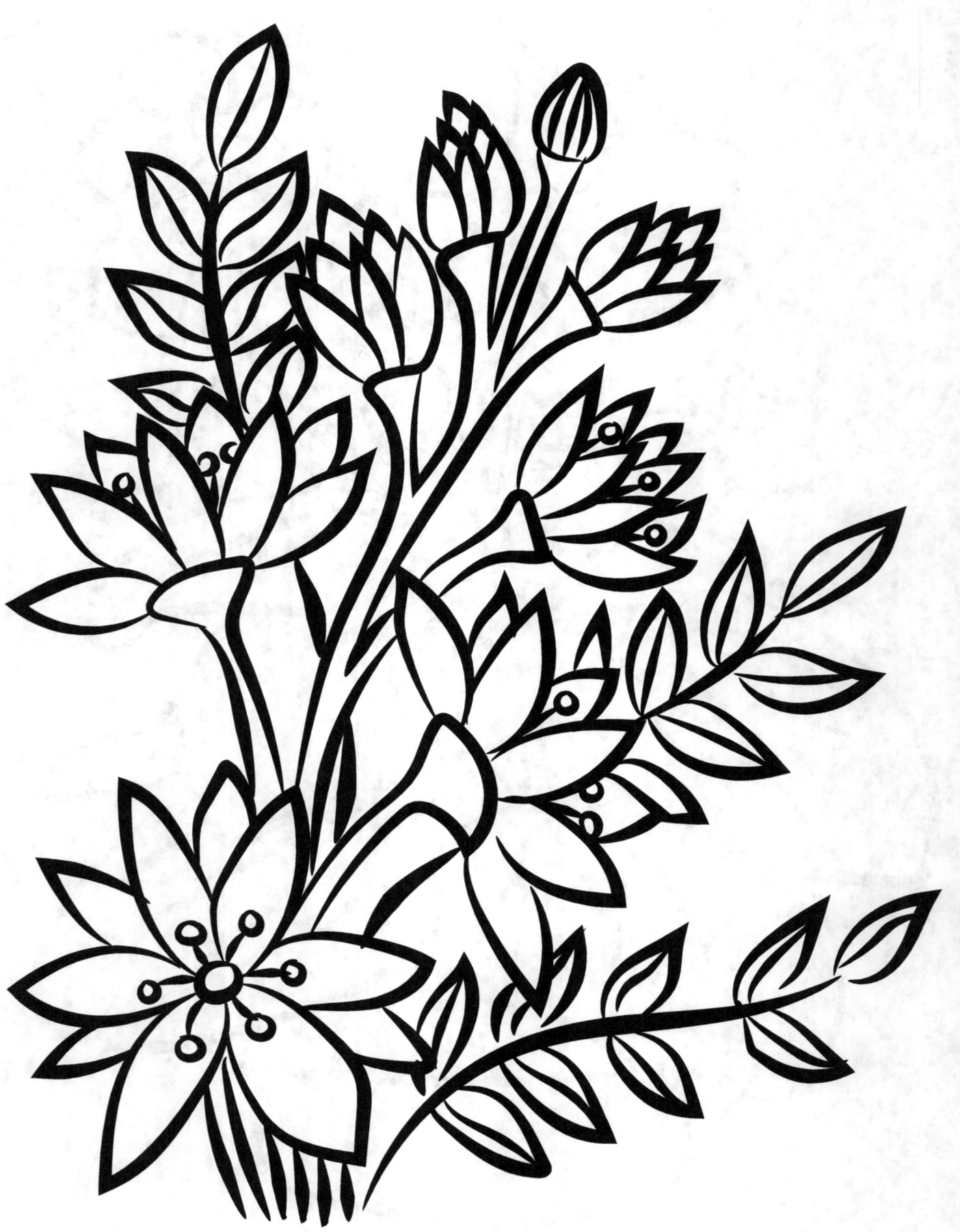

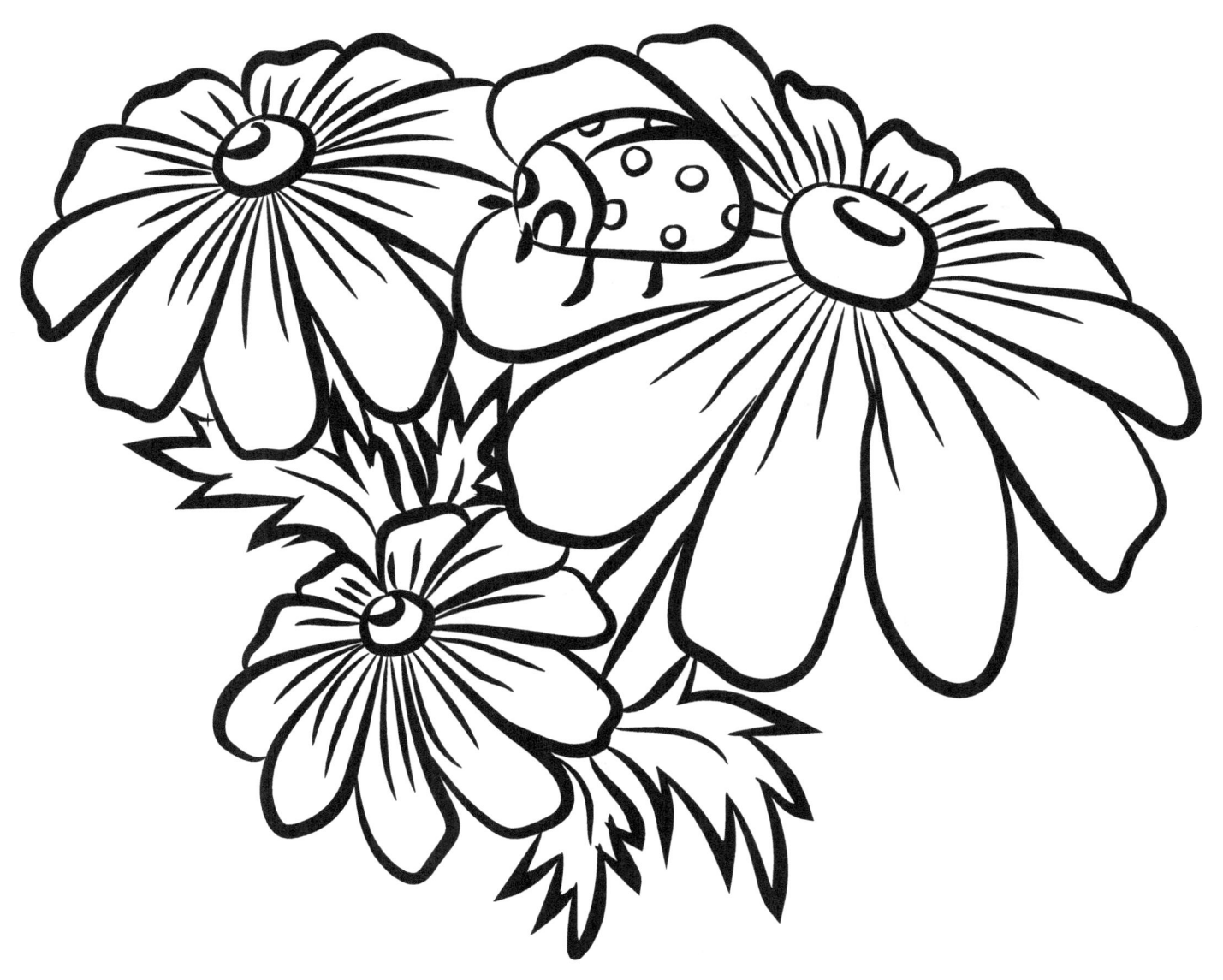

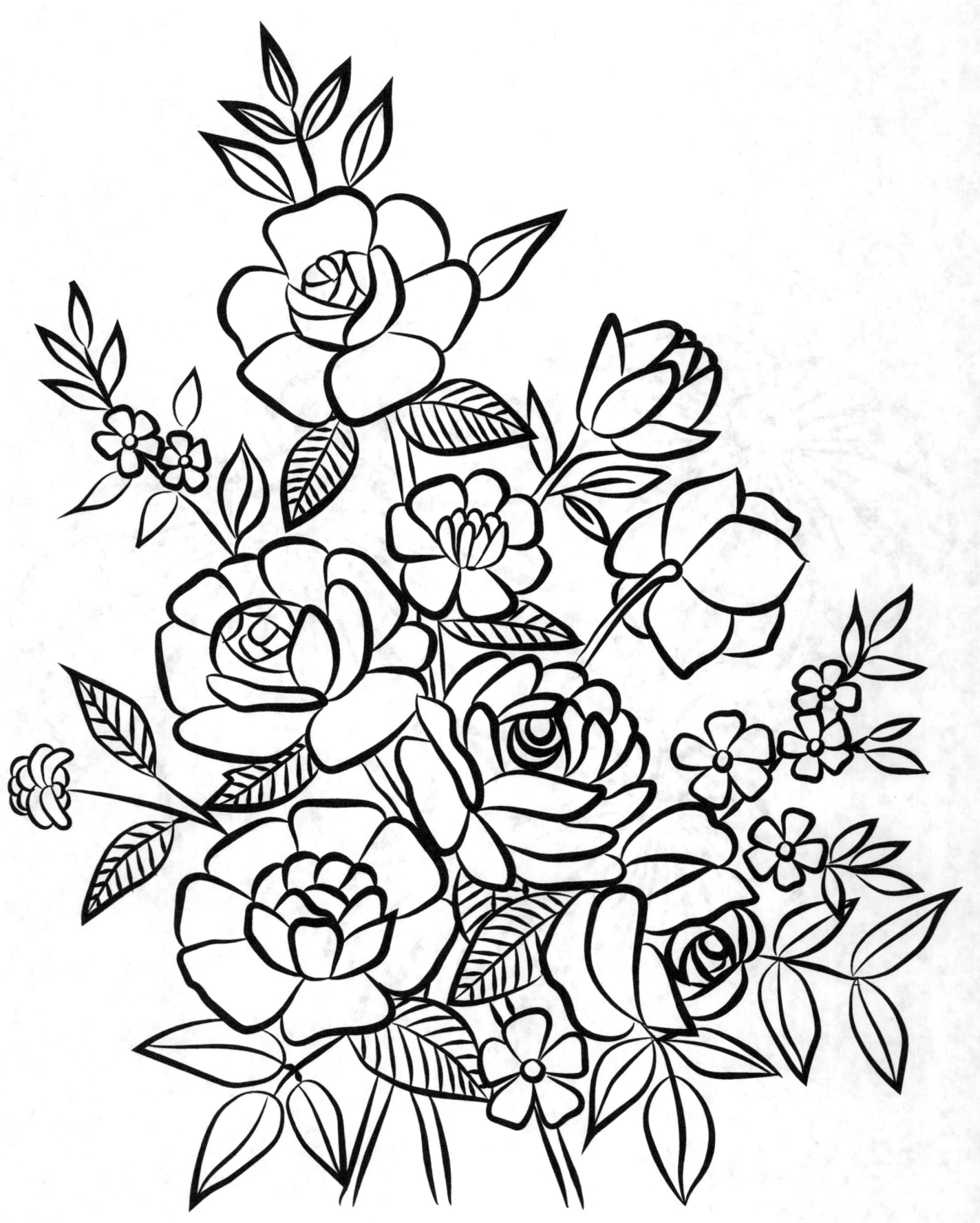

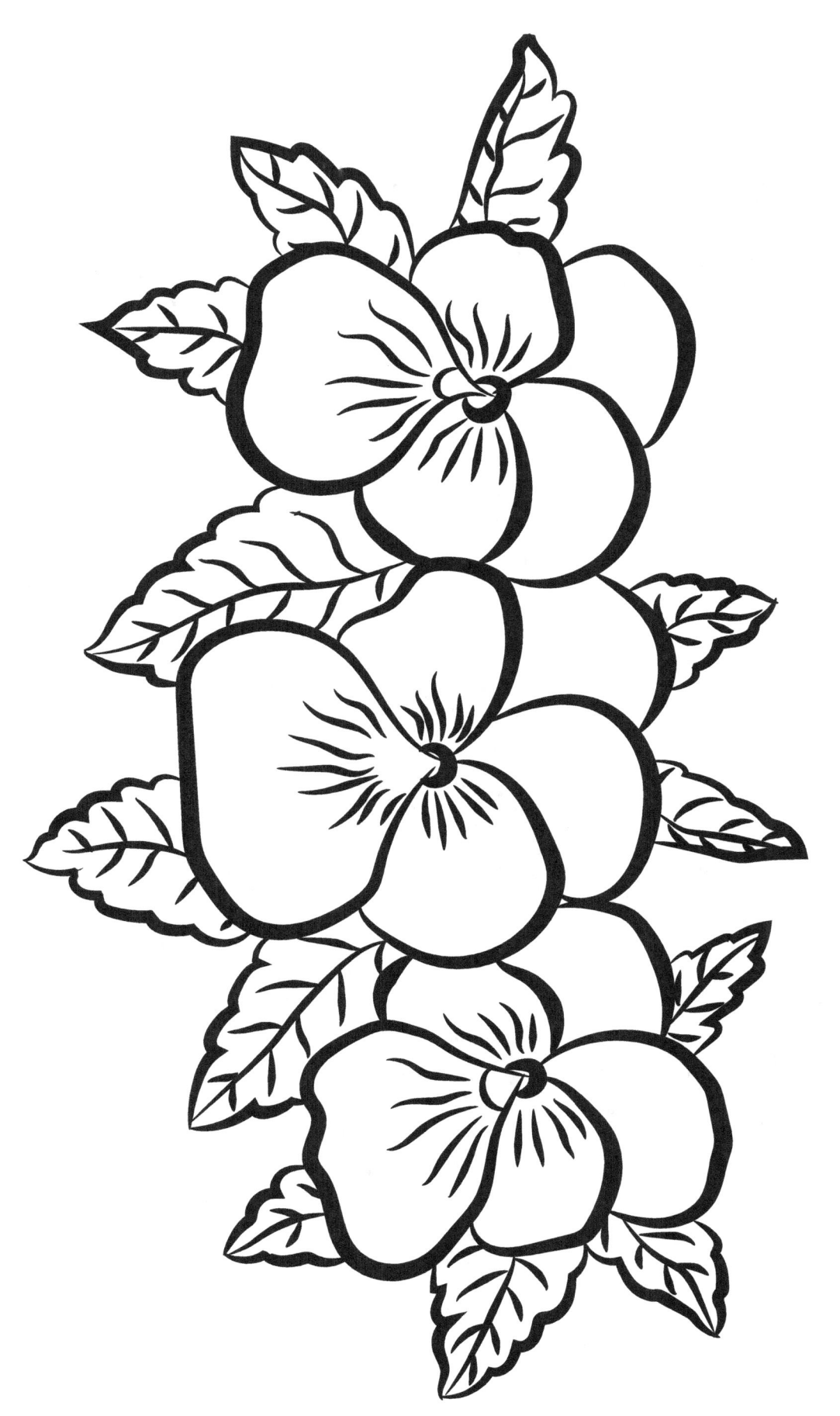

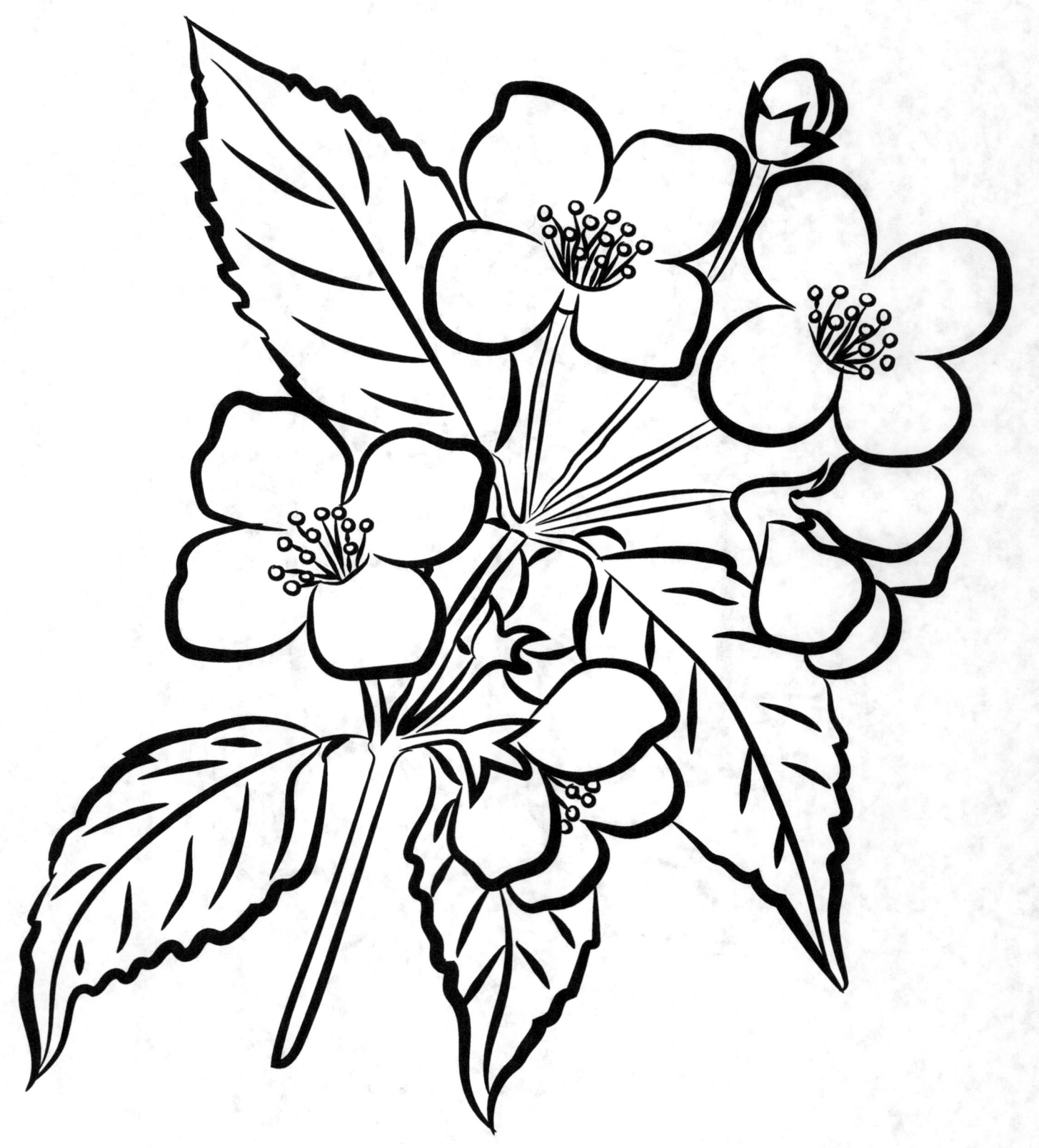

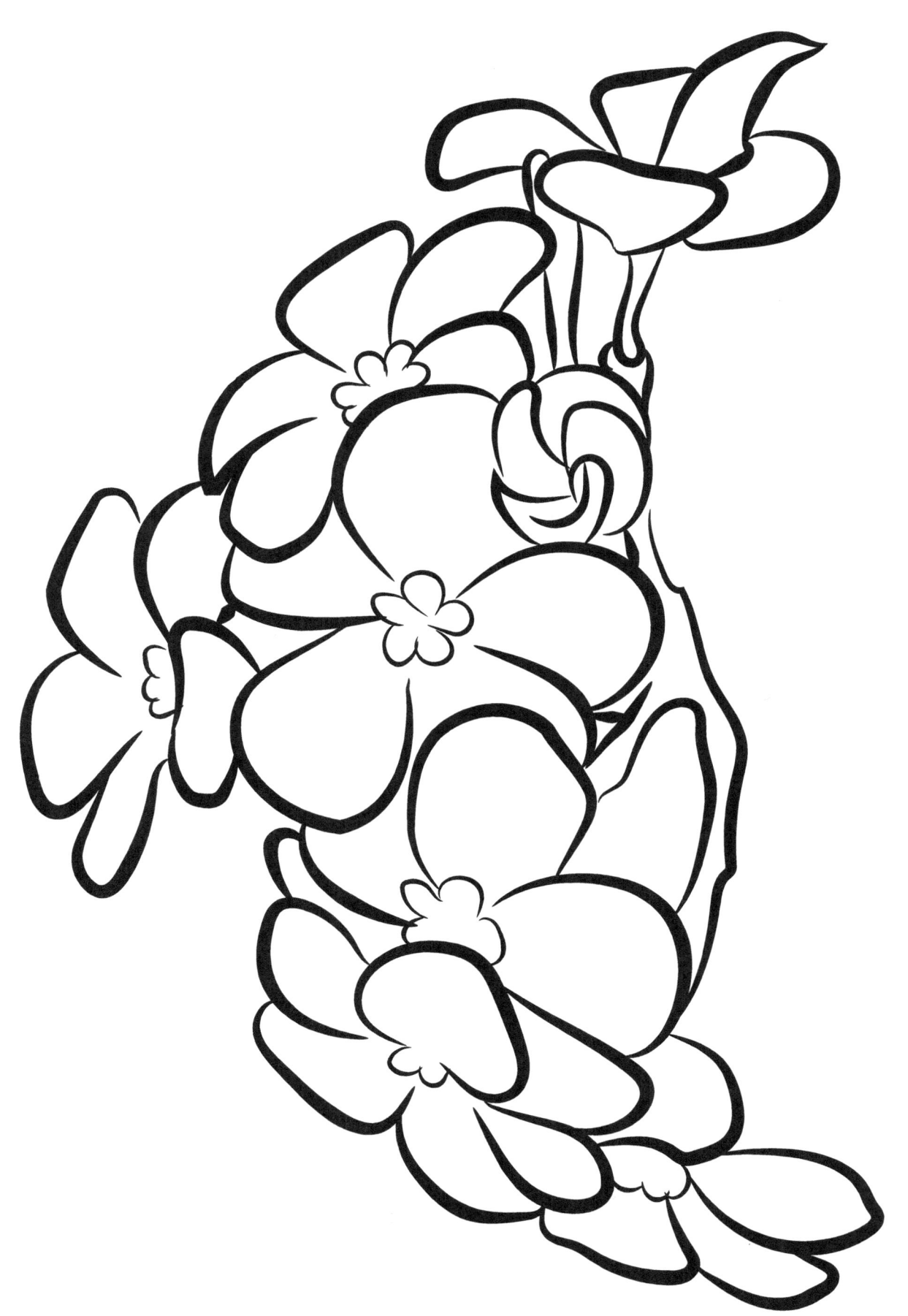

ISBN-13: 978-1719574631
ISBN-10: 1719574634

www.ingramcontent.com/pod-product-compliance
Lightning Source LLC
Chambersburg PA
CBHW060005230526
45472CB00008B/1962